The Kindness of Strangers

D0104704

The Kindness of Strangers

*Adult Mentors, Urban Youth,
and the New Voluntarism*

Marc Freedman

CAMBRIDGE
UNIVERSITY PRESS

PUBLISHED BY THE PRESS SYNDICATE OF THE UNIVERSITY OF CAMBRIDGE
The Pitt Building, Trumpington Street, Cambridge, United Kingdom

CAMBRIDGE UNIVERSITY PRESS
The Edinburgh Building, Cambridge CB2 2RU, UK   http://www.cup.cam.ac.uk
40 West 20th Street, New York, NY 10011-4211, USA http://www.cup.org
10 Stamford Road, Oakleigh, Melbourne 3166, Australia

Copyright © 1993 by Jossey-Bass Inc., Publishers, 350 Sansome Street,
San Francisco, California 94104. Copyright under International, Pan
American, and Universal Copyright Conventions. All rights reserved.
No part of this book may be reproduced in any form – except for brief
quotation (not to exceed 1,000 words) in a review or professional
work – without permission in writing from the publishers.

First published by Jossey-Bass Inc. 1993.
This paperback edition published by Cambridge University Press in 1999.

Printed in the United States of America

*A catalog record for this book is available from
the British Library.*

Library of Congress Cataloging-in-Publication Data
Freedman, Marc.
The kindness of strangers : adult mentors, urban youth, and the
new voluntarism / Marc Freedman.
p.   cm.
Includes bibliographical references and index.
ISBN 0 521 65287 1
1. Volunteer workers in social service – United States.   2. Urban
youth – Services for – United States.   3. Voluntarism – United States.
I. Title.   II. Title: Mentors, urban youth, and the new voluntarism.
HV91.F684   1993

ISBN 0-521-65287-1 pb

for
Bud Freedman, Mike Bailin, and Gil Stott,
mentors all

Contents

Preface

*Time and time again I have been persuaded that a huge
potential of goodwill is slumbering within our society.*
— Václav Havel,
Summer Meditations

Many Americans care deeply about the fate of young people
growing up in poverty. We worry about their future and that
of an increasingly fragmented society. We would like to make
a difference, yet this yearning is so often stifled by the sheer
magnitude of social problems and by the absence of mechanisms
for reaching out. We want to help, but frequently don't know
how to do so, or even where to begin.

In this context, mentoring has emerged as a vehicle for
translating yearning into action. Mentoring not only provides
a conduit for action but a way to think about acting; rather than
take on the overwhelming weight of urban issues, mentors are
afforded the opportunity to connect with a single individual.

Furthermore, mentoring springs from a compelling,
common-sense insight. Young people in our society, across the
socioeconomic spectrum, are not getting enough caring or

personal attention from adults. Increasingly, they are growing up alone and forgotten. Nowhere is this condition more trobling than in the case of inner-city youth, who confront far greater stress than their contemporaries of higher social and economic status.

The Kindness of Strangers tells the story of the concerned adults who have come forward to mentor these youth, one-to-one, in cities across the United States. It seeks to illuminate what middle-class volunteers, focused on forming personal relationships, can do to ameliorate the conditions of young people living in poverty. In telling the story of mentors and youth, the book also chronicles the rise of the mentoring movement and examines its wider implications for education and social policy.

I began working on this book in 1988, at a time when voluntarism and voluntary movements were being upheld as a substitute for public policy. George Bush was waxing about "a thousand points of light" and warning that "bureaucracies cannot soothe the shuddering body of a crack baby or act as mentor to a throwaway child." Americans were offered the choice of a "good" or a "Great" society: the former based on private acts of goodwill; the latter characterized by expensive and ineffective public institutions.

The points of light message carried with it some intuitive appeal – in its emphasis on responsibility for others and its critique of bureaucratic impersonality – but the call for private action in the context of government inaction also engendered legitimate concern. The call to help was urgent and warranted, yet the altruism of individuals was being used to justify neglect of essential public institutions.

Against this backdrop, and in the context of a new administration in Washington intent on integrating the "good" and "Great" societies, *The Kindness of Strangers* presents mentoring as a vivid illustration of how voluntarism can not only complement government efforts but contribute to broader institutional revitalization.

While volunteer mentors won't singlehandedly meet all the interpersonal needs of American youth, mentoring highlights the importance of adult relationships for youth while challenging us to move beyond voluntarism and to implement structural changes capable of increasing opportunities for adult contact in the schools, community organizations, and social programs where young people spend so much of their time. As such, volunteer mentoring amounts to the citizen-participation wing of a broad and promising movement to personalize education and social policy.

However, mentoring is of essential importance not only for its direct contribution to youth but also for its effect on many volunteers. At a time when statistics have lost their ability to shock, mentors are brought face to face with the unfair manner in which poverty affects innocent children. Some begin to ask, "What would I do under these circumstances?" On the heels of empathy comes commitment, and many mentors are moved to advocacy. While it won't be easy, mentoring programs can provide an opportunity to build on these sentiments and to generate public support for essential and humanizing reforms.

For all these reasons mentoring constitutes, in the words of one volunteer, "a window of hope," a glimpse not only of our better selves but of a potentially better society, one built not only on individual acts of kindness but on a broader set of programs, policies, and institutions that themselves reflect a higher civility.

Berkeley, California MARC FREEDMAN
July 1993

Acknowledgments

While the principal concern of *The Kindness of Strangers* is the fate of young people in poverty, its main protagonists are middle-class adults – the individuals who have initiated and promoted mentoring programs and have come forward to "do good" under often challenging circumstances. The mentoring movement is built on the kindness, courage, and commitment of these strangers. Their voices echo throughout the book, and the extended reflections of eight reside in sections entitled "Answering the Call" at the end of Chapters One through Eight. My profound appreciation goes to all these individuals, as well as to the many young people who took time to talk with me openly and at length about their experience with the one-to-one process. At root, the book is an attempt to pass on what they told me.

The Kindness of Strangers exists because of funding from the Ford Foundation, and I am deeply indebted to Robert Curvin, director, Urban Poverty, for his encouragement and support.

The book also exists because of Michael Bailin and Gary Walker of Public/Private Ventures. They championed this effort from beginning to end, helped me develop my ideas, and provided the time to complete the book. In short, they've been my mentors on this project, and I could ask for none better. I'd like also to express gratitude to a set of colleagues at Public/Private Ventures for their help: Mary Achatz, Alvia Branch, Mike Callahan, Jim Connell, Catherine Furano, Jeff Greim, Rodger Hurley, Maxine Sherman, Cindy Sipe, Tom Smith, Lois Snodgrass, Melanie Styles, Joe Tierney, Dine Watson, and Joe Zakrzewski.

My profoundest thanks go to Natalie Jaffe and Carol Thomson, who edited an earlier version of the manuscript and provided friendship, good humor, and intellectual stimulation throughout the writing process. Special thanks go as well to another set of friends and advisers who offered expertise and support at many critical junctures: Rachel Baker, Brooke Beaird, Bill Bloomfield, Isabel Bradburn, Erik Butler, Ray Chambers, Richard Danzig, Paul DiMaggio, Joy Dryfoos, Jane Lee Eddy, Erwin Flaxman, Nancy Florence, Karen Fulbright, Frank Furstenberg, Rob Gurwitt, Andy Hahn, Betty Hamburg, Steve Hamilton, Lisa Hicks, Alex Hoffinger, Doc Howe, Vania Laveille, Dan Levitt, Joan Lipsitz, Margaret Mahoney, Dagmar McGill, Tom McKenna, Mary Phillips, Delia Pompa, Jane Quinn, Jean Rhodes, Carol Rothstein, Joan Schine, Lee Schorr, Cathy Ventura-Merkle, Heather Weiss, and Emmy Werner.

Particular appreciation goes also to the dedicated entrepreneurs and staff at mentoring programs who shared their time and thoughts while opening up their programs to me. Shayne Schneider of Mentors, Inc., Buzzy Hettleman of Project RAISE, Marcienne Mattleman of Philadelphia Futures, Cathy Munson of One-on-One, and Al Abromovitz and Marsha Mockabee of Cleveland Career Beginnings not only taught me about mentoring but offered friendship in the process.

Finally, I'd like to thank Lesley Iura, Marcella Friel, Currie McLaughlin, Patricia O'Hare, and Laura Simonds at Jossey-Bass for their advice, encouragement, and support.

M.F.

Introduction
to the Paperback
Edition of
The Kindness of
Strangers

Five years ago in the hardcover edition of *The Kindness of Strangers*, I argued that mentoring was "a window of hope," a way of providing the adult caring and personal attention that many young people desire, a model for the kind of humanizing reforms needed in the schools and other settings where children spend much of their time, and a potential vehicle for expanding adult advocacy on behalf of the young people most in need.

For all these reasons the book was optimistic about the potential of mentoring. It was also my hope that *The Kindness of Strangers* might serve as a call to action, inspiring more adults to come forward to serve as responsible mentors. Yet, in the book, and in other forums, I worried that mentoring might be undermined by the "fervor without infrastructure" practiced by some of its partisans, that it might turn out to be just another oversold and passing fad.

Five years later, I am happy to say, the mentoring movement is alive and growing. Without discounting the earlier concerns – which remain concerns today – I am heartened by several developments that have occurred since *The Kindness of Strangers* first went off to press.

Emerging Lessons

Most important, we now know a great deal more about the potential value mentoring and mentoring programs can have on young lives.[1] Some of this knowledge derives from major research studies examining young people in their communities, outside the context of formal mentoring programs. The first wave of findings from the largest study of adolescent health ever done, the $25 million National Longitudinal Study of Adolescent Health that surveyed 90,000 students in grades 7 through 12, is a powerful example.

Published in *the Journal of the American Medical Association* in September 1997, these findings underscore the central importance for young people of relationships with caring adults both within and outside families. Furthermore, the Adolescent Health study makes it clear that the actual messages adults impart to youth are less critical than the simple fact that they spend time talking to them and showing them they care. According to Dr. Robert Blum, a professor of pediatrics at the University of Minnesota and the study's principal investigator, what matters most is "that there is a sense of caring and connectedness that comes through from at least one person in school, from a parent, from someone, that really protects kids from all sorts of negative outcomes."[2]

The Adolescent Health study followed closely on the heels of the largest investigation of community violence ever done, conducted by researchers at Harvard, Chicago, and Michigan State and published in *Science*. Looking at neighborhoods in Chicago with similar socioeconomic circumstances but dramatically different rates of violent crime, researchers found that the differences could be attributed, more than anything else, to adults taking a direct interest in the lives of kids. In particular, the neighborhoods with lower crime rates were places where adults were more willing to intervene directly in the lives of youth, especially when they violated the norms of the community.[3]

At the opposite end of the scale from these studies involving tens of thousands of youth, recent research probing deeply into the lives of small samples of children is producing similar conclusions. One of the most compelling examples is a study of 24 young people from impoverished neighborhoods who made it to Ivy League universities, by Arthur Levine, dean of Teachers College at Columbia University. Levine, like Blum and numerous earlier researchers in the field of resilience, makes it clear that mentoring is an important common denominator in the lives of children who manage to avoid the temptation of the streets and achieve success in mainstream society.[4]

The past five years have also seen an upsurge of research demonstrating the importance of caring adult contact in the context of youth programs. One example is the Quantum Opportunities Program, a demonstration project funded by the Ford Foundation and conducted in four cities around the United States. A front-page story in *The New York Times* heralded the results from this effort – produced through a random-assignment study adhering to the strictest standards of social science research – as "some of the most remarkable results for poor youths since the test runs for Head Start." According to the evaluation of this program, a chief reason for these gains was the close relationships forged between young people and adult youth workers who mentored them through the program. As one of the youth involved explained, "With an entire support system rooting for our success, it was more difficult to give up."[5]

The Big Brothers/Big Sisters Study

While all these new studies contribute to the body of literature suggesting that mentoring matters, none more vividly supports this view than Public/Private Ventures' 1995 study of the Big Brothers/ Big Sisters program. It was a study that grew, in part, out of the research for this book. In performing research for *The Kindness of Strangers*, I visited the leadership of Big Brothers/Big Sisters.

Although the primary purpose of my meeting was to learn about their views on the growth of the mentoring movement, at the end of our session Big Brothers/Big Sisters officials asked whether Public/Private Ventures – the non-profit research organization where I was based – might be interested in an evaluation of the program nationally. I was stunned: After nearly 100 years of matching "Bigs" and "Littles," why would this organization suddenly be interested in an evaluation? They had never needed one in the past to attract either volunteers or monetary support.

The answer was that the great growth in upstart mentoring programs making overheated claims about what they would be able to accomplish – in numbers and impact and at little cost – was prompting tough questions from prospective funders around the country, including many United Ways. Local Big Brothers/Big Sisters projects, in turn, were urging the national organization to undertake the kind of research that might enable them to respond appropriately to these questions. A match was soon made, and in 1992, before *The Kindness of Strangers* was even published, an independent evaluation, funded by a consortium of national foundations, commenced.[6]

To carry out the research, Public/Private Ventures studied nearly 1,000 ten- to sixteen-year-olds who applied to Big Brothers/Big Sisters in 1992 and 1993 but were still on a waiting list. More than 60 percent of the sample were boys; more than half were members of minority groups, mostly African Americans. More than 80 percent came from impoverished families, and almost all were being raised by a single parent, usually the mother. Approximately 40 percent were from homes with a history of drug or alcohol abuse and nearly 30 percent came from families with a record of domestic violence.

Half these young people, randomly chosen, were matched with a Big Brother or Big Sister, while the rest stayed on the waiting list. Eighteen months later, the differences between the two groups were dramatic. The involvement of a Big Brother or Big Sister in a young person's life for a single year reduced first-time drug use 46 percent (at a time when drug use is mounting among teenagers), cut school absenteeism by 52 percent, and lowered violent behavior by 33 percent. Youth with a Big Brother or Big

Sister were more likely to perform well in school, much more likely to relate well to family and friends, less likely to assault somebody, and much less likely to start using alcohol. The effects were sustained for both boys and girls and across races.

What was especially startling about these findings is that the mentors were not trained in drug prevention, remedial tutoring, antiviolence counseling, or family therapy: Their instructions were to gain the kids' trust and become their friends. A companion study that looked in-depth over 18 months at 82 Big Brothers/Big Sisters relationships concluded that those adults who could carry out those instructions – not those determined to "straighten these kids out" – were far more likely to gain the trust and time necessary to have an influence on youths' lives.

After nine months, more than 90 percent of those mentors who paid attention to the young person's need to have fun and who simply took the trouble to listen to the youth, were meeting regularly with the Little Brother or Sister. Only 30 percent of mentors who were out to transform the young person's life through prescribing goals and emphasizing behavioral changes were still meeting at all. In short, the mentors who didn't try so hard to make a difference – but who are simply there for the kids – managed to make all the difference.

The other important factor in the success of mentors studied in the Big Brothers/Big Sisters research, as well as in other programs, appears to be an intensive and consistent time commitment. Although there is individual variation, in most cases it takes approximately six months of meeting ten hours or more a month for the adult volunteers to establish trust.

Other research, including studies of mentoring for teenage mothers by Jean Rhodes, a psychologist at the University of Illinois at Urbana-Champaign, also points to consistency on the part of mentors as a key factor in connecting with inner-city kids and making a difference in their lives. Rhodes' research, looking at both mentoring that occurs naturally in communities and mentoring that is developed through programs, suggests that "the rich do get richer." In other words, young people with the capacity to find mentors on their own, outside of the context of formal mentoring programs, also make the best use of mentors they are provided through programs. However, Rhodes also finds that many young people without the internal wherewithal to find mentors can be reached through formal programs. The key appears to be not only consistency on the part of mentors, but persistence: a willingness to forge ahead despite seeming indifference on the part of young people in the early stages of the relationship.[7]

These discoveries are enormously encouraging, as encouraging as the findings concerning mentoring's impact on young people. They underscore that one does not need to be either charismatic or a sage to succeed at this enterprise: What's most important is lending young people an ear and showing up on a consistent, persistent basis.

The Road Ahead

With some key common-sense insights and powerful evidence of effectiveness now lined up behind mentoring, it would seem time to forge ahead and dramatically expand the number of mentoring relationships available to the young people who need them most. Unfortunately, two obstacles stand in the way, obstacles that were present five years ago and that remain significant today. They are the number of adults available to serve as mentors and the organizational resources necessary for carrying out a successful program.

Available Adults

For all of Big Brothers/Big Sisters' success, the program is too small – far too small – in comparison to the number of young people who want or need a mentor. It currently has a waiting list equivalent to nearly half the number of youth it matches, a list comprised disproportionately of African-American boys. Estimating that 5 million to 15 million children could benefit from a Big Brothers/Big Sisters match, one Big Brothers/Big Sisters official laments: "We're not coming anywhere near to meeting that need."

In part, that modest number of 75,000 Big Brothers/Big Sisters' matches results from a careful and lengthy screening process; only about one in four people who show initial interest actually become mentors. But that care is critical, not simply to screen out pedophiles but because relationships that don't work can be damaging to kids. It's important to know if an interested, well-meaning adult really has the time to mentor (the Big Brothers/Big Sisters mentors Public/Private Ventures studied met with their kids on average three times a month, 3.5 hours each time – that's 126 hours a year, or about three 40-hour work weeks).

There are a multitude of smaller mentoring programs around the country, and there is no current reliable estimate of the number of mentors they deploy or the time those mentors put in. But if the findings of an earlier Public/Private Ventures survey hold up, a generous estimate is that these many smaller efforts now triple the Big Brothers/Big Sisters number. Given the estimate of the number of kids who could use mentoring, it seems reasonable to conclude that *at best* a small percentage of kids who could benefit from mentoring are getting it.[8]

Infrastructure and Resources

Though some Americans would like to believe that doing good springs simply from the heart, the Big Brothers/Big Sisters experience suggests that, at least in the case of mentoring, making a genuine difference requires a great deal more. It takes persistent, consistent involvement, and, as already noted, that necessitates substantial care in recruiting, screening, matching, and supporting the volunteers. In the case of Big Brothers/Big Sisters, these critical functions are carried out by paid caseworkers. As a result, the program costs, on average, $1,000 per year per match.

The practices and cost of Big Brothers/Big Sisters are not to be taken lightly. As part of a broader study of mentoring, Public/Private Ventures examined a number of other mentoring programs that are much less structured, and thus much less costly, than Big Brothers/Big Sisters. These studies found far fewer "successful" relationships, of much shorter average length – and many more adult volunteers who were ill-prepared for the commitment and empathy required in mentoring a young stranger.[9]

Perhaps the Big Brothers/Big Sisters results can be achieved for something less than $1,000 per year – but it won't be free. If we're very generous and mark the new, streamlined mentoring at $500 per year – and use the lower figure of 5,000,000 kids in need – we're still about $2.5 billion short.

The Mentoring Summit

In April 1997, in the midst of profound shortages of volunteers and dollars in the world of mentoring, a "President's Summit for America's Future" was convened in Philadelphia. The event drew Presidents Clinton, Bush, Carter, and Ford and was led by retired General Colin Powell. These luminaries were joined by 30 governors from both major parties, half the members of the Clinton cabinet, numerous Congresspersons and Senators, and thousands of others. The goal of the Summit: to provide 2 million children with mentors, safe places, health care, job skills, and the opportunity to perform community service. However, the emphasis on providing caring adult volunteers for these youth was the original goal of the event and remained so prominent that the convocation in Philadelphia was frequently depicted as "the mentoring summit."

History will tell whether the Summit amounts to more than a massive exercise in "fervor without infrastructure." A year and a half later, the jury is still out. In April 1998, the *Washington Post* reported that the goals were not close to being realized. Focusing on the location of the event, the *Post* wrote: "What is known in Philadelphia, where the summit began, is that the single most important goal – connecting needy children with caring mentors, tutors and coaches – is far from being realized." Only 12,000 mentors had been found for the 120,000 young people the city had pledged to match with adult volunteers. *The New York Times*, in a Summit follow-up article, observed that "there is little evidence as yet of masses of individuals coming forward nationwide."[10]

Clearly, the Summit goals were unrealistic from the start – and to a fantastic degree. After nearly a century of operation, Big Brothers/Big Sisters has not yet exceeded 100,000 matches. How could we possibly add 2 million more individuals, in a responsible manner, in the three and a half years between the Summit and the millennium?[11] Nevertheless, it appears that some good has come from the event. Hundreds of businesses have donated money and employee time toward the goals of the Summit. For example, Pillsbury, in a particularly noteworthy effort, pledged more than a million dollars to Big Brothers/Big Sisters programs in locations where the company has a presence and made mentoring relationships with children a priority for all its employee volunteer programs.

There has also been a steady drumbeat of public affairs announcements emphasizing the importance of mentoring and highlighting findings from mentoring research, especially the Big Brothers/Big Sisters findings. Dr. Jay Winsten, director of the Center for Health Communications at Harvard's School of Public Health and originator of the Designated Driver campaign, is developing a campaign to increase the number of mentors. The campaign's message appears to be a responsible one, emphasizing that mentoring requires real commitment and a holistic approach: "Rather than focusing on discrete problems such as drugs, alcohol, dropping out of school and youth violence, all of which may affect the same child," states Winsten, "the strength of mentoring is that it deals with all those problems simultaneously by addressing the needs of the child as a whole."[12]

Another encouraging sign is the leadership and commitment of Colin Powell. Initially many questioned whether Powell's role in the event was politically motivated. Others wondered whether he would quickly move on to different pursuits after the Summit limelight passed. Despite these reservations, and many post-Summit organizational difficulties, it seems clear that General Powell was being honest when he promised that he was "in this for the long haul." And his leadership has extended well beyond pushing more mentoring, as he continues to serve as a spokesman for Boys and Girls Clubs and to emphasize the importance of service opportunities for young people.[13]

As important as committed leadership, a responsible message, and increased corporate support are, we are unlikely to be able to close the mentoring gap without substantial new infusions of public funding devoted to helping strengthen and expand the programmatic infrastructure. As a recent UPS Foundation – sponsored study shows, 40 percent of adults who volunteered pre-

viously stopped because the organizations where they served
made poor use of their time. It is not enough to ask for more
mentors; we must provide high-quality programs capable of chan-
neling their goodwill in responsible ways.[14]

Here too, however, there are some hopeful signs. In Congress, Democrat Frank Lautenberg of New Jersey successfully
shepherded the Juvenile Mentoring Program Act (JUMP) to pas-
sage, providing federal support for grassroots mentoring programs. JUMP has also won the hearts of some conservative
Republicans. In 1996, then-Senator Dan Coats of Indiana – who
along with Connecticut liberal Chris Dodd is one of two former
Big Brothers in the Senate – announced that he would include a
measure based on JUMP, the Character Development Act, as one
of 18 bills in his Project for American Renewal. Coats' act proposed offering federal grants to link public schools and local
mentoring programs. Former Republican Governor Pete Wilson
of California proposed putting state funding directly into local
mentoring programs for the purpose of finding a way to confront
teenage alcohol and drug abuse, pregnancy, violence, and school
failure. Delaware has also launched a statewide mentoring initiative.

But these hopeful signs are only that; on balance, most policy efforts remain small, scattered, and symbolic.

Stocking the Pond

Blending public and private support would enable mentoring programs like Big Brothers/Big Sisters to better address youths' need
for adult contact and strengthen the support available to adults
who provide that contact. Still, as *The Kindness of Strangers* argues,
it would be a mistake to either underestimate the extent of these
needs or overestimate the power of volunteer efforts to meet them.

The isolation of young people is a structural problem
resulting from fundamental, corrosive changes in our society. We
will need to move beyond volunteers if we are to make a genuine
dent in the problem. From where might these reinforcements
come? For one, we need to expand the number of part- and full-
time paid youth workers available to connect with children as

mentors, in school and during non-school hours. The Quantum Opportunities Program is but one example of how this strategy might pay off. Hugh Price of the National Urban League esti-mates that we could support 500,000 such youth workers for the crucial afternoon/early evening hours for the price of the 100,000 new police officers that were such a central part of the Clinton Crime Act.

In fact, this vision of a "small army" of adults committed to youth is being partly realized through national service, another example of the role public policy can play in rebuilding the social capital available to kids. A significant portion of AmeriCorps' national service participants are working in direct and intensive one-to-one roles with youth, many of them helping to expand grassroots mentoring projects.

Friends of the Children in Portland, Oregon, offers a com-pelling example. Created by a local financier, the program employs "full-time caring, loving adults" who each work inten-sively with eight young children identified by teachers as destined for trouble. The adult Friends spend time in the classroom, serve as a bridge between school and home, and act like surrogate fam-ily to the kids. Their goal is to stick with them from second grade through high school. Until two years ago, however, budget restrictions limited this promising program to four adult friends. With AmeriCorps dollars, Friends of the Children moved from a complement of four to a corps of twenty-four mentors, and the number of children served increased dramatically.

The Experience Corps is another promising initiative. This effort, funded by the National Senior Service Corps and an array of private foundations, mobilizes a critical mass of neigh-borhood retirees serving in paid full-time and half-time and unpaid part-time positions to help transform local elementary schools into more caring and personal places. The project oper-ates entirely in low-income communities and was recently expanded to YMCAs, Boys and Girls Clubs, and neighborhood libraries. The Experience Corps members provide intensive one-to-one attention for young people in these institutions, recruit parents to become more involved in the schools, and help develop enrichment activities both before and after school.

Ultimately, as the Experience Corps suggests, if we hope to develop more powerful strategies for supporting kids we must strive to combine the efforts of volunteers and nonvolunteers in ways capable of transforming the two settings where young people spend the majority of their time outside the home: schools and youth organizations. This is particularly urgent at a time when so little of the money, public and private, being spent on reform of youth-serving institutions – public schools, foster care, social services – results, as an intermediate outcome, in more sustained adult contact with youth. Currently only a few of these reform efforts focus on adult contact and guidance.

In contrast, our goal should be to work through schools and youth organizations to construct a web of support for children, a portfolio of adults acting together, as partners, to help out with the long-term, complex process of developing young people. Ultimately, as the ensuing book argues, this approach dictates changing schools and youth programs so that these become places where youth encounter an array of caring adults. In creating *mentor-rich* environments, we will need to fill them not only with volunteer mentors, who constitute an important link in the chain of caring, but also with youth workers, teachers, coaches, counselors, and other adults with the time and inclination to establish close ties with young people.

As we go about creating more humane climates in these institutions – essentially "stocking the pond" with interested adults in a variety of capacities – we might simultaneously work to develop the capacity of youth "to fish," to make the best use of the adults they find in their path. Doing so builds off a central lesson from the study of resilient children – that these young people overcome poverty through actively *recruiting* mentors from the surrounding community. We might well strive to distill and teach recruitment and relationship-building skills to a wider spectrum of kids.

Pursuing a combination of these strategies would move us dramatically past the prospects of volunteer programs alone and would help us to begin reconstructing the social infrastructure our young people so desperately require.

Civilizing Society

If we succeed in keeping community volunteers as an important part of this mix and recruiting them in ever-increasing numbers, we might do something else as well: help renew civic life in this country. Yet another major development occurring since publication of *The Kindness of Strangers* with implications for mentoring is the emergence of an important national debate about civic engagement in America. Triggered by publication of Harvard political scientist Robert Putnam's 1995 essay, "Bowling Alone," this debate has drawn attention to the overall decline in volunteerism since the late 1980s (from 54 to 49 percent during the period 1989 to 1995, according to a Gallop Survey for the Independent Sector) as well as the decline in specific forms of service, such as PTA membership, which has slipped from 12 million to 7 million since the 1960s. Putnam's title derives from his discovery that while bowling in this country has increased in recent years as a recreational pursuit, bowling leagues are on the decline – a decline he sees in other forms of membership activity as well.[15]

In this context, the emphasis on more Americans coming forward to volunteer as mentors is particularly welcome, especially because face-to-face volunteering on behalf of the needy is one of the most underrepresented forms of service. And mentoring brings an amusing twist to the civic engagement debate: It turns out that bowling constitutes one of the most lucrative sources of fundraising dollars for Big Brothers/Big Sisters projects around the country – through a fundraising vehicle called Bowl for Kids' Sake. With endorsements from both the Professional Bowlers Association and the Bowling Proprietors of America, two million Bowl for Kids' Sake participants produce more than $15 million a year for Big Brothers/Big Sisters. Since 1981, bowling fundraisers have generated more than $125 million in donations for the mentoring program.

Will mentoring prove to be an important part of a new wave of civic activity in America? Will it be a stimulus toward reconstructing a constituency for children and youth in this country?

Will it serve to help improve the lives of significantly more young people over the coming decades? These questions continue to loom large, as they did when this book was first published. In conclusion, I can say that the past five years have revealed the central role mentoring can play in both social policy and civil society. Mentoring has truly shown itself to be a window of hope, one with the potential to illuminate many future paths.

Notes to the Introduction

1. Much more is also known about corporate mentoring, a field that continues to grow and evolve. However, because the main focus of *The Kindness of Strangers* is on mentoring for young people living in poverty, new research in the corporate sphere is not covered in this introduction. For more information, however, one article worth consulting is "Earning It: Mentoring Meets Networking in Formal Programs," *The New York Times,* November 30, 1997.

2. Resnick, Michael, and others, "Protecting Adolescents from Harm: Findings from the National Longitudinal Study on Adolescent Health," *Journal of the American Medical Association*, September 10, 1997, pp. 823–832; Gordon, Debra, "Caring Adults 'Innoculate' Teens Against Risky Behavior," *Youth Today*, November/December 1997, pp. 26–7.

3. Sampson, Robert, and others, "Neighborhoods and Violent Crime: A Multilevel Study of Collective Efficacy," *Science*, August 15, 1997, pp. 918–24.

4. Levine, Arthur, and Nidiffer, Jana, *Beating the Odds: How the Poor Get to College* (San Francisco: Jossey-Bass, 1996).

5. See citations in Schorr, Lisbeth, *Common Purpose* (New York: Doubleday, 1997), pp. 3–5; Dugger, Celia, "For Young, a Guiding Hand Out of Ghetto," *The New York Times*, March 9, 1995; Hahn, Andrew, "Evaluation of the Quantum Opportunities Program (QOP): Did the Program Work?" Brandeis University, June 1994.

6. The following account and other sections of this new introduction draw heavily on Walker, Gary, and Freedman, Marc, "Social Change One on One," *The American Prospect*, July–

August 1996, pp. 75–81; also see Sipe, Cynthia, "Mentoring: A Synthesis of P/PV's Research: 1988–1995" (Philadelphia: Public/Private Ventures, 1996).

7. Conversations with Professor Jean Rhodes, Department of Psychology, University of Illinois at Urbana-Champaign.

8. See Sipe, "Mentoring: A Synthesis of P/PV's Research: 1988–1995."

9. See Sipe, "Mentoring: A Synthesis of P/PV's Research: 1988–1995."

10. Havemann, Judith, "A Year After Summit, Volunteer Effort Falls Short of Vision," *Washington Post*, April 26, 1998; Miller, Judith, "Push for Volunteerism Brings No Outpouring," *The New York Times*, September 23, 1997; Dundjerski, Marina, and Hall, Holly, "General Powell's Charity Gets Mixed Reviews from Non-Profit Leaders," *Chronicle of Philanthropy*, April 23, 1998.

11. For one local example of overselling, see: Miller, Judith, and Johnston, David Cay, "Critics Say United Way Plan Can't Meet Goals for Children," *The New York Times*, December 24, 1997.

12. Elliott, Stuart, "All Aboard the Campaign for a Few Good Mentors," *The New York Times*, November 7, 1998.

13. Alter, Jonathan, "The Nicer Nineties," *Newsweek*, December 29, 1997; Johnson, Dirk, "Powell's Youth Drive Gains Steam After Sputtering," *The New York Times*, June 14, 1998; Powell, Colin, "Recreating the Civil Society – One Child at a Time," *Brookings Review*, Fall 1997; Dundjerski, Marina, and Hall, Holly, "America Answers Call to Help Kids," *Chronicle of Philanthropy*, April 23, 1998.

14. Morin, Richard, "Don't Waste the Volunteers' Time," *Washington Post*, May 18, 1998. Also see Lewin, Tamar, "In Search of a Cause: Volunteering Dos and Don'ts," *The New York Times*, December 9, 1997.

15. Putnam, Robert, "Bowling Alone: America's Declining Social Capital," *Journal of Democracy*, January 1995.

1

A Call
to Action

If one saves a single life,
it is as if one saved an entire world.
—The Talmud

On April 19, 1989, *Washington Post* columnist Dorothy Gilliam issued a wake-up call to the decent people of Washington, D.C., challenging them to open their eyes, roll up their sleeves, and join in a battle to win back the hearts of the inner-city youth.

"Who will answer the SOS?" she asked, as more and more innocent youth are swept into the vortex of drugs, gangs, and violence. Who will come forward before another generation of disadvantaged children is lost to the streets?

Gilliam's plea was triggered by the arrest of drug dealer Rayful Edmond III. According to the police, Edmond controlled 20 percent of the district's drug trade, while his gang was suspected of thirty murders. In the process, Gilliam reported, Edmond had become a folk hero on the streets of Washington, particularly to young people growing up in impoverished and isolated urban neighborhoods.

1

In issuing her SOS, she urged readers to take responsibility for thousands of innocent young people poised at a crossroads, who every day must fight to avoid active involvement with drugs. Without intervention, Edmond and his compatriots would be the only heroes many youth would ever have the chance to know. "We cannot let the drug dealer replace the rest of us as role models," Gilliam argued. "More than ever today we have to be the keeper of our brother's children."

The first step toward assuming responsibility would need to be a new awareness on the part of the mainstream models whose lives suggested the importance of other routes — education, hard work, responsibility, and restraint. Repelled by what was happening in the inner cities and unwilling to subject their own children to urban hazards, these positive models had erected a wall between themselves and "the drug thugs," often retreating to outlying enclaves where urban poverty remained out of sight and out of mind.

But a new awareness would just be the start. Action would also be required, and in the current environment of suburban flight and government cutbacks, Gilliam stressed, it would not be possible to wait for someone else to act. What would be needed is the radical step of "each one teach one."[1]

Specifically, Dorothy Gilliam's call to action was a call *to mentor,* to win hearts through forging "regular, hands-on, one-to-one, relationships" with youth fighting against the odds and in jeopardy of not making it. Some mentoring efforts were already underway in Washington churches and civic organizations, but their numbers were too small. If thousands of youth were going to be saved, if another lost generation was going to be averted, these efforts would have to be doubled, even quadrupled.

In conclusion, Gilliam recalled the words of Rabbi Hillel, "If I am not for myself, who will be for me? And if I am only for myself, what am I? And if not now — when?"

A total of fifty-five individuals answered. Together they adopted the banner "SOS Volunteers," and, promising to get together with young people in poverty once a month, they joined forces with an already existing program, Mentors, Inc. By fall, the SOS Volunteers were being matched, one-to-one, as mentors to students at Washington's McKinley High School.

The Rise of Mentoring

Dorothy Gilliam's SOS, while particularly compelling, was by no means a lone cry. In Washington and elsewhere across the country, a growing chorus of mentoring appeals could be heard. Just four days earlier, the *New York Times* had described a set of new one-to-one initiatives engaged in a "tug of war for black youths' hearts," offering a picture of young people so isolated they were like "canoes floating in the ocean without a compass." The article quotes Howard University sociologist Joyce Ladner, who states that many inner-city youth "need three or four parents sometimes just to stay on top of what's happening to them every day. . . . That's why mentors are so important."[2]

One of the earliest testimonies to mentoring's importance can be found in the 1983 annual report of the Commonwealth Fund, a New York philanthropy. The report begins with an essay titled "Mentors," written by the Fund's president, Margaret Mahoney, which argues that young people have lost "natural proximity to caring, mature adults," leaving their "basic need for constructive guidance" unfulfilled. This problem is portrayed as particularly acute for children in poverty, who, "living in scarred, deprived neighborhoods . . . confront too many negative influences, too many bad models." Stating that one-to-one relationships "can reassure each child of his innate worth, instill values, guide curiosity and encourage a purposeful life," Mahoney concludes that mainstream adults in America must come forward and devote "a small but significant part" of their time to mentoring disadvantaged youth.[3]

The Commonwealth Fund began supporting mentoring projects in the early 1980s, including one effort in New York that matched disadvantaged youth with mentors from the Coalition of 100 Black Women. This initiative evolved into a national project called Career Beginnings, soon operating in two dozen cities.

Despite Commonwealth's leadership and its willingness to help fund the mentoring cause, it was not until the late 1980s that mentoring took hold as a movement. In 1989, the influential William T. Grant Commission on Work, Family and Citizenship, with Hillary Rodham Clinton as one of its members, recommended that "many more mentoring programs be developed, evaluated, and refined, especially those that involve young people in ongoing relationships based on shared purpose and mutual interest."[4] At approximately the same time, President George Bush taped a television commercial endorsing mentoring, and it was declared one of the first initiatives of the Points of Light campaign. On the other side of the political spectrum, New York's first lady, Mathilda Cuomo, declared 1989 to be "The Year of the Mentor."[5]

By 1990, a range of highly influential organizations and corporations, including Chrysler, Procter & Gamble, IBM, the United Way of America, the National Urban League, and the National Education Association, were aboard the mentoring juggernaut. At the same time, philanthropist Raymond Chambers created One to One to stimulate mentoring in communities around the country, while another new entity, One PLUS One, began promoting these efforts on television and in the press. In March, the first National Mentoring Conference was sponsored by private foundations, corporations, and the U.S. Department of Labor. Later that year, the United Way cosponsored another national conference, with speeches from the president and other prominent figures.

By the summer a rapid multiplication was underway at the local level. Observing this growth Shayne Schneider, the founder of Mentors, Inc., the Washington, D.C. program with which the SOS volunteers affiliated, noted that "there were twice as many programs last year and twice as many programs the year before and the year before."[6] The movement swelled in most major cities and many smaller ones, with efforts ranging in size from a handful of mentors to over a thousand. Some programs focused on young people on the verge of dropping out, while others offered enrichment to those performing reasonably well in school. Some mandated weekly personal contact, while others stretched the definition of mentoring to include only monthly phone calls. The common denominator throughout was an emphasis on recruiting middle-class adult volunteers to forge one-to-one connections with disadvantaged youth.

Schneider's Mentors, Inc., offers one illustration of the

process. Operating in all D.C. high schools, it focuses on low-income students "in the middle," not likely to drop out but in jeopardy of falling short of their potential. The program draws mentors from Washington's vast business and professional community and is involved in a formal partnership with the city's Board of Trade, the chamber of commerce for large corporations. By its third year, Mentors, Inc. was overseeing five hundred one-to-one matches.

In nearby Baltimore, Project RAISE offers a contrasting mentoring model. Initiated by Bob Embry, president of the Abell Foundation, it focuses on young people in danger of dropping out, graduates of seven of the city's most disadvantaged elementary schools. Through RAISE, seven organizations — two churches, two banks, two colleges, and an African-American fraternal organization — each adopted a class of sixth-graders, promising them one-to-one mentors through high school graduation. The project's goal is to reduce the dropout rate among participants by 50 percent.

Like Mentors, Inc. and Project RAISE, many of these new initiatives are the product of efforts by social entrepreneurs working in a wide variety of settings. Surveying the mentoring landscape, it is possible to locate several particularly rich sources for programs.

One of the most fertile has been the African-American community. Many organizations have initiated projects focused on linking inner-city youth with successful African-American men and women, individuals who, in many cases, were themselves raised in inner-city neighborhoods and attended urban public schools. In Providence, Rhode Island, the local Urban League started the Education Initiative Program, providing approximately one hundred students with mentors for three years. In Oakland, California, the Frick Mentoring Program matches African-American women professionals with teenage girls. In Philadelphia, the Omega Psi Phi fraternity is providing mentors as part of a scholarship program sponsored by a retired Philadelphia school administrator. In Pittsburgh, Milwaukee, and many other cities, local chapters of One Hundred Black Men are matching African-American men and youths in one-to-one relationships.

The corporate world has been another wellspring of mentoring programs. As part of the upsurge of business's interest in education over the past decade, many corporations have gone from adopting schools to encouraging employees to "adopt" individual students. In Milwaukee, the business community launched the citywide One-on-One effort, involving Blue Cross, local utilities, city government, the Rotary Club and other institutions in efforts to mentor at-risk middle school students. In Cincinnati, Procter & Gamble is sponsoring Project ASPIRE, a program that matches one hundred students from low-income Woodward High one-to-one with Procter & Gamble employees.[7] In Austin, Texas, IBM manages Project Mentor, with the "simple premise [that] giving young people consistent, one-to-one support and attention — that is, serving as a friend and role model — boosts self-esteem, increases work quality, and, most of all, improves school attendance."[8] Elsewhere, numerous corporations and businesses, small and large, are active in these efforts.

Private organizations have not been the only contributors to this new field. On the public side, a number of states are actively involved in stimulating mentoring. One of the first efforts was the New York State Mentoring Committee under the leadership of Mathilda Cuomo. Minnesota later set up a Governor's Task Force on mentoring and youth service, while California created an office of Mentoring and Youth Services. The most ambitious state-level undertaking is Rhode Island's Children's Crusade. The crusade focuses on low-income third-graders who qualify for the school lunch program. They are promised scholarships for college and offered mentors drawn from the state's senior citizen, college student, and working professional populations. The Children's Crusade aims to help disadvantaged minority kids stay in school, specifically to "reduce the dropout rate to an unacceptable-but-improved 25 percent from a horrendous 50 percent."[9]

Emanating from social entrepreneurs, community organizations, corporations, and government entities, a full-fledged field of mentoring programs now exists, most of it initiated since the late 1980s. While it is not possible to pin down precisely the number of programs or volunteers in a quickly changing environment, these new efforts appear at least to equal in size the on-going efforts of Big Brothers/Big Sisters, which nationally main-tains seventy thousand matches. Furthermore, the new crop of mentoring efforts is serving primarily young people in poverty.

Acknowledging this new wave of activity, the *Philadelphia Inquirer* editorialized in December of 1989 that mentoring had become "downright trendy," declaring that "as the Helmsley-Boesky era ends, the fresh interest in youth is a reason for hope."[10] The *New York Times* later proclaimed "an enormous surge" in men-toring programs, observing that "in recent years, the idea of directly contributing to a youngster's chances of success has found great appeal among educators, business leaders and others."[11] And the *Baltimore Sun* pronounced: "Mentoring—in which some-one who has made it helps along someone who hasn't—suddenly has become hot among educators and others trying to solve high dropout rates among inner-city youth."[12]

Along with the 1990s, mentoring had arrived. Built around the elements of middle-class voluntarism, personal relationships, and a focus on poor children, this movement could claim not only a wide range of supporters and a burgeoning field of new programs but considerable optimism about what it would soon accomplish.

At the Crossroads

When Dorothy Gilliam invoked the fate of innocent youth poised at a crossroads, she was calling out for volunteers to help young people like Sean Varner. A student at McKinley High School, the school where the SOS volunteers came forward to serve, Sean's situation was desperate.

Not only fatherless but homeless, Sean spent his first year of high school living in a shelter. The sixteen-year-old, his mother, and four siblings resided in a single rat- and roach-infested room, with a hot plate serving as their kitchen. Sean had his own bed, his little brother and sister shared a bed, and his baby sister and mother shared another, while Sean's older brother slept on the floor. Eventually, the situation became unbearable: "I had, like, a little breakdown," Sean states. "One day my little brother just got to me. I wanted to take things out on him. I got to the point where I was just so angry — at him, at a lot of things — I just sat there and cried."

Later that year the Varners moved to a transitional shelter while more permanent quarters were being arranged. The new building, at Fourteenth and Park Row, was an improvement over the previous shelter, but its location was actually worse — in the middle of a thriving drug market. Each day on the way home from school, Sean walked past a procession of drug dealers prodding him, "Are you ready yet? You ready yet?"

His younger brother answered in the affirmative and was soon spending time in jail. Sean's older brother was not involved in drugs but dropped out in junior high school after being held back three times.

In the tenth grade, Sean contemplated dropping out. He stopped going to school, but after several weeks of failing to find work he unenthusiastically drifted back to McKinley. His attendance sporadic, his grades were a mix of incompletes and failures, punctuated by an occasional B or C.

All this time, however, Sean was actively reaching for help. At school he latched on to a sympathetic guidance counselor, Ruth Taylor: "I was always in her office, all the time, reaching out, looking for someone to be in my corner." Taylor liked Sean and saw potential in him. She was justified. He would soon score the highest PSAT scores at McKinley — despite poor attendance and grades, homelessness, and poverty — and qualify for National Merit Scholarship consideration.

Taylor wanted to help Sean but with a caseload in the hundreds, realized she couldn't provide the kind of individual attention and support he was seeking. Furthermore, she felt that Sean, who'd seen his father only once, needed a male presence in his life. When the counselor heard about the Mentors, Inc. program, she made sure Sean applied and shepherded him through the process.

In a few weeks, Sean was matched with a mentor, John Hogan. Hogan closely fit Dorothy Gilliam's description of decency — responsible, church-going, a physician married to another physician. Sean was astonished by how much the thirty-seven-year-old Hogan, born and raised in rural Georgia, looked like Martin Luther King, Jr.: "He had that accent, and I was looking at his facial features, and that's what I thought."

Initially, John tried to find some common ground with Sean by recounting his own background: growing up poor, one of eleven children. All Sean could think about was how elated he was just to have "someone to sit down and listen to me—to give me a chance to talk." While adults were frequently coming in and out of Sean's life (recently his godparents had started visiting), they tended to "preach" to him. With John there was no preaching. Sean recalls that from the very beginning, "we would go to a restaurant and sit there and just talk. I was real down on myself, dealing with a whole lot of problems I shouldn't have been dealing with, which he helped me get off my back."

Within a few months, Sean and John's relationship evolved from a formal match—essentially a blind date—to something resembling extended kinship. According to Sean, "Out of everyone I know, John's my best friend. If the mentor program were to blow up tomorrow and be gone—no more mentor program—we'd still have our relationship."

Through talking to John, Sean feels he's been able to stabilize his life emotionally: to get perspective, to keep from blowing up at teachers, and to remain focused on the goal of graduating from McKinley and going on to college. Sean credits this support, guidance, and encouragement with "a tremendous jump" in his life. For the first time, his grades and school performance reflect the potential evident in his standardized test scores. Although Sean is convinced he would have eventually landed on his feet even without John's help, he adds, "It would have been too late, schoolwise . . . and even then, it would have been a lot harder."

John Hogan's reflections on meeting and mentoring Sean follow. They are joined, after each of the subsequent chapters, by the accounts of seven other mentors, each in his or her own words. These personal narratives are designed to anchor the arguments presented in the chapters, to give voice to some of the most articulate commentators on the mentoring process, and to convey the wide diversity of mentoring experiences. They offer a vivid reminder that mentoring is, at root, about the efforts of real people to connect across what is often a great social divide.

Answering the Call

John Hogan is a volunteer with Mentors, Inc., in Washington, D.C. He is matched with Sean Varner, a student at McKinley High School.

I was looking for a program where I could help young people. In sports I root for the dynasties—whoever's on top—but for people, personal things, it's the ones that are having a tough go of it that I care about, and that's kind of the way I see myself, doing things the hard way but not giving up, and not letting people know that things may not be so smooth.

I'm from a little town in Georgia, in the country. I grew up going to segregated school—my one school went from the first through the twelfth grade. My oldest brother was my mentor; he was internally motivated. But in high school I had an opportunity to go to Phillips Academy in Andover for the summer. There I met people from all over the United States trying to do something with themselves, and our conversations focused on college—"Where you gonna go to college?"—and I had to think fast, because I'd never thought much about it. This experience really changed my life. And that summer I saw Brandeis University, and I said, "This is where I want to go."

I came to Brandeis that next fall wanting to be a doctor, but like so many of the other black students, by the end of the second year, I'd been wiped out. I had just about given up. And one day during my junior year I was walking across campus talking to one of my math professors, and he asked me, "John, what do you really want to do?" And I said, "I'd really like to be a doctor, but I'm afraid it's just too late." He couldn't believe it. He said, "John, don't ever give up on your dream. If you want to be a doctor then you go

11

for it, even if you have to go back to school after you graduate. But if that's what you want, on the inside, don't let anybody dissuade you."

And it was like that day did it for me, that one day, that one conversation. And I went back to school, and things worked out. But having had my own ups and downs, it gives me a little extra insight, sometimes, into what Sean's going through.

When I signed up for the program I got this piece of paper in the mail with Sean's name and number on it. I dialed the number and the person on the other end said, "CMS Shelter." And I said, "Ah, oh, I'm sorry, I must have the wrong number," and hung up. So I pulled out the paper again, looked at the number, and called back, and the person answered again, "CMS Shelter," and maybe I said, "Excuse me," and hung up and tried one more time. Finally I said, "I'm trying to get in touch with Sean Varner," and the person told me that she couldn't give out the number of residents, because I had reached a shelter for homeless people. She said, "Here's the name of somebody you can call back tomorrow."

I immediately called my wife and told her, "This is over my head. This guy lives in a shelter. I don't see how I can relate to someone coming from that situation." But she calmed me down, said she had faith in me, that it would probably be okay. I had just completely written myself off as not able to communicate with Sean. I knew I wasn't going to get some upper-middle-class kid—but I figured at least it would be somebody that lived in an apartment, or in the projects. Homelessness is something that you see all the time in Washington, but it just hadn't touched me personally like that.

The next day I called back and the woman I spoke to was so enthusiastic about what I was doing, so I went forward. I went to the school to see Miss Taylor, the counselor, who knows Sean. We talked about his living situation and she showed me his grades, which were not good at all at that time. He was thinking about quitting school. He'd missed so many days, and all I saw was D's and C's and F's.

12

I met Sean for the first time right here, in this room [in the school]. We just small-talked, about how many people were in his family, things he was interested in outside of school, just breaking the ice. The first thing I had to do was listen to him. I needed to know what he thought and felt about certain things, about what he wanted, versus bombarding him with a lot of junk.

But Sean made it easy. He reached out from the very beginning. He called me, made it easy to get in touch. Sean wanted someone to be there for him, somebody to believe in him, to motivate him.

It's funny, that first meeting I asked him what kind of student he was, and he said, "I'm an A student." And I thought to myself, this guy better wake up—I had seen his grades—I couldn't believe he was that cocky. I thought, Who do you think you're fooling? But he showed me: now he's an A student, honor roll, highest PSAT scores in the school.

He's exactly the kind of student this program is designed to reach, the ones with lots of potential, but who, for whatever reasons, are getting lost. Basically Sean has done all the work, all I do is try to get him to focus and keep him goal-oriented. He gets upset with the teachers and doesn't want to do the work. I say, "Wait a minute, wait a minute, you're at a point where you need the grade, brother, so you don't have time to rebel, you have to keep your mind on what you're doing." Miss Taylor, the counselor, also helps a lot, and Shayne [Schneider, who runs the mentoring program] helps too. They'll let me know when he's running into trouble.

I started out getting together with Sean half an hour a week. Now it's much more informal. When I get the chance I come by and we'll just go to McDonald's, or if I'm going to visit some friends, and I'm going to be near his house, I go by and say, "Come on, Sean, come ride with me." This is my way of keeping in contact. It's also a way of introducing him to someone else who's doing something with his or her life, not just in medicine but whatever else it is that they're doing. It's a way to keep him motivated, to give him that push.

We talk a lot about what it takes to survive in life, about dealing with situations that are coming up in his life, interactions with people, with Miss Taylor, his Spanish teacher, his mother, me.

We're friends. We're not mentor and student anymore, we were for a month or two, but then we got hooked. But I'm hard on Sean, too. There are a lot of things I feel he needs in a hurry, especially if he's gonna try to leave here and go away to school. I often find myself asking him to make changes in his life that I'm trying to make in mine — to be an adult or to do adult things that me and my wife and our friends are all trying to grapple with ourselves — and he's eighteen years old!

But Sean's unique. I don't think there are many Seans in this or any program. The things he has faced. The dynamics in his house. It's just incredible what he has survived. I just have to shake my head each time [I go to his place]. But he just keeps moving forward. I have so much respect for him: for what he's faced, for what he's dealing with — for what he's not giving in to.

2

Great Expectations

One-to-one mentoring of youth has proven to be a
low-cost, high-yield solution that pays off.
—Lynn Martin,
former U.S. Secretary of Labor

*B*uoyed by stories like Sean Varner and John Hogan's, the rise
of mentoring has been accompanied not only by a flurry of activity but also a great fervor about what this movement will accomplish in alleviating the problems of disadvantaged youth.
Laying out the stakes, the One to One Foundation tells us: "Our
nation today faces some of the most serious human and social
problems in its history." In response, the foundation offers mentoring as "the best hope."[1]

Keynoting the first National Mentoring Conference, former Secretary of Labor and Red Cross chief Elizabeth Dole sup-
plies historical import, reminding her audience that the individuals who founded this country "did so at a risk to their very
lives." In turn, she asserts, we are required "by history to give
ourselves . . . to the call of mentoring," which "can keep kids in
school, turn young lives around, impact on the social problems

15

of our time, improve the quality of our work force, and ensure America's continued competitiveness." Calling mentoring a "great force," Dole concludes that this collection of benefits isn't "a bad day's work."[2]

Senator Frank Lautenberg adds to the list, contending that mentoring can "build self-esteem, keep youngsters in school, improve academic skills, increase the child's ability to seek and keep jobs," while further "preventing drug abuse, teen pregnancy, illiteracy, unemployment and welfare dependency." Mentoring programs, Lautenberg concludes, "have already shown they can change children's lives."[3]

Commonwealth Fund president Margaret Mahoney asks, "Is there any greater challenge for the individual adult in America today [than] serving as a mentor?"[4], while John Pepper, president of Procter & Gamble states, "I am absolutely convinced there is nothing any of us can do that is of greater importance than *mentoring* for helping our youngsters develop to the fullness of their abilities."[5]

Millions of Mentors

With similar zeal, mentoring's proponents have promised ranks befitting a great force. The magic number for the current movement is one million volunteers, although some have suggested even greater participation. One foundation executive argues that former President Bush "had the right idea, but the wrong mathematics," and has called for "several million 'points of light.'"[6]

Another leader of the movement, Frank Newman, president of the Education Commission of the States, explains the urgency of realizing such a goal, stating that mentoring is one of five strategies that "works . . . over and over and over again, essentially for every child." With this perspective, he identifies the number of mentors needed: "We looked at the research information and came up with the figure: a million. A million every year. A million mentors a year, because a million kids come along every year who need mentors."[7] In this vein, the Department of Labor initiated a project challenging five thousand businesses to ante up 10 percent of their employees as mentors.[8] The

One to One group has set the objective of not only a million mentors nationally but one hundred thousand in Philadelphia alone.[9]

Turning Lives Around

Sold as a mass movement, mentoring is also portrayed as a powerful force in the case of individual lives. An article in the *Washington Post,* "Turning Young Lives Around," illustrates this perspective through an account of John Hogan and Sean Varner's story. The piece begins by describing the youth's predicament: "Sean Varner's family lived in a shelter for the homeless. The teenager owned few clothes, was failing in school and considering dropping out. Then John Hogan entered his life." After eighteen months, "With Hogan's encouragement and support, Varner turned his life around," resulting in vast improvement in grades, attendance, and aspirations: "A host of colleges are courting him. His conversations are peppered with talk about his future, about college and a career as an engineer."

Arguing that Sean's transformation is typical of the mentoring experience, the article concludes: "What happened to Sean Varner illustrates how concerned adults are touching the lives of troubled youth around the country through mentoring programs. It's the perfect answer for a generation of people who have time to volunteer and a desire to help solve some of the problems plaguing young people in inner cities."[10]

In their manual for mentoring, *Partnerships for Success,* the United Way of America and the Enterprise Foundation supply another archetypal mentoring story, that of Evelyn and Paige: "Not long ago, Evelyn could not read or write. She was the third generation of her family to become dependent on welfare. Her children seemed likely to repeat the pattern." However, Evelyn explains that her life began to change the day a friend referred her to Literacy Volunteers, a United Way agency that connected her to Paige, a mentor from the other side of the tracks. Evelyn states: "I needed a person out there to help me because I did not know all the people who could help me stay off welfare."

Soon things began to turn around: "Over the months,

Evelyn's skills and confidence began to grow. She learned how to get help as well as to solve her own problems. Progress wasn't easy. Some of Evelyn's 'friends' on welfare questioned her actions, put her down, even threatened her. But with the support of Paige, and her sympathetic welfare caseworker Louise, Evelyn moved ahead." Eventually, Evelyn became assistant manager of a corporate cafeteria. According to *Partnerships for Success,* the story of Evelyn and Paige "summarizes what can happen when one caring individual volunteers to mentor another."[11]

The *Oakland Tribune* adds a third story to the canon, describing Vincent Piper's mentoring efforts on behalf of young Dennis Tomlinson. "'Dennis was doing poorly in school, getting bad marks in citizenship and generally not living up to his ability,'" the article quotes Piper. But then the mentor stepped in and laid down the law: before the pair did any "fun things . . . [the student would] have to improve his grades." Although at first all Dennis did "was sit there and pout," the article goes on to report, "Last semester, Tomlinson, now fifteen, achieved a 3.0 grade point average for the first time. 'I couldn't believe it,' he said, a shy grin spreading across his face. 'I used to just sit around and watch TV.'"[12]

The Mythology of Mentoring

The excitement that surrounds mentoring takes its strength from these stories and builds through sweeping claims about the scale on which it can work. Both the larger vision and the individual success stories contribute to an overarching mythology about what mentoring and mentoring programs will accomplish. Stepping back from these claims and stories, it is possible to distill a set of key elements that make up the new mythology.

A Source of Success — and Salvation

Most prominently, mentoring is cast as a powerful vehicle for individual success. We are repeatedly told that mentoring will impart self-esteem, improve SAT scores, break the cycle of welfare dependency, and generally reaffirm the principle, to quote the title of a *Harvard Business Review* article, that "everyone who makes it has a mentor."[13] The United Way of America's mentoring partnership with One to One is called "a success strategy for youth," while a newspaper headline describes mentoring as "the pied piper of success."[14]

But mentoring is not just about success of the incremental sort but about dramatic, resounding, life-transforming success. Sean is brought from the brink of dropping out to the heights of academic achievement; Evelyn moves from the welfare rolls to the ranks of management; Dennis is elevated from TV fiend to honor student.

Essentially, mentoring is depicted as child saving. Echoing Dorothy Gilliam's invocation of mentoring as the way to save thousands of lives, Judge Randolph Jackson of the New York State Supreme Court adds that mentoring is not only a route to "serve" youth, but to "save" them — in particular, the minority youth he frequently sends to prison for drug dealing, robberies, and other crimes.[15] In this process of salvation, mentors are portrayed not only as good-hearted but as heroic. An advertisement for mentoring in the *Philadelphia Inquirer* tells potential mentors that they hold "the power to change lives,"[16] while Thomas Evans, chairman of the board of Teachers College, Columbia University, invokes a string of examples illustrating mentors accomplishing "miracles."[17]

Revitalizing American Competitiveness

The claims accompanying mentoring are not restricted to effecting individual success. Proponents, in portraying a mass movement of millions, raise the stakes to the level of America's competitive success in the international economy.

Elizabeth Dole promises that mentoring will "improve the quality of our workforce and ensure America's continued competitiveness." David O. Maxwell, CEO of Fannie Mae, states that mentoring will solve our need for "skilled workers,"[18] while Mathilda Cuomo agrees that mentoring "can do a lot" to fill this "dire need."[19] Former Xerox Chairman and Deputy Secretary of Education David Kearns explains that mentoring is a route to turning "this country's brain drain into a brain gain."[20] Advocates specifically point to the power of mentoring to combat the circumstances of the most disadvantaged. According to One to One's Philadelphia action plan, it will combat "the emergence of a permanent underclass."[21]

A Cheap and Easy Solution

Whether working at the individual or societal levels, mentoring is further portrayed as a cheap and easy route to success, a "quick fix" to long-standing and vexing social problems, a "low-cost, high-yield" solution.[22] In the low-cost vein, mentoring is frequently offered as an opportunity to bypass institutions and head directly to individual solutions. One to One reminds us that "just as the ultimate victims of poverty are individuals, so too the ultimate solution lies in the actions and values of individuals . . . reaching out to those in need *One to One*."[23] Norman Brown, president of the Kellogg Foundation, testifies that "the greatest need of young people today is not another program, but another caring, loving human being" as a mentor or role model.[24] Senator Lautenberg argues that it is "a low cost way" to help children "break the cycle of poverty and despair."[25]

At the same time, mentoring is depicted as easy. One program tells mentors it is "easy to make a difference in one kid's life."[26] Another adds, "The time you spend is just four hours per month. The students are willing participants. Their parents are supportive. Success is practically guaranteed."[27] A newspaper article states that time is "all it takes to give a kid the lessons of a lifetime."[28]

The Heroic Conception of Social Policy

Upheld as the "ultimate solution," the "perfect answer," a "great force," a "quick fix," lauded as cheap, easy, widespread, focused on the most disadvantaged, and capable of transforming lives dramatically, mentoring is promised as a strategy equal to such considerable challenges as maintaining American competitiveness in the twenty-first century. These characterizations convey an enthusiasm that stands out even in the fad-bound arena of social policy.

Mentoring's fervor is rooted in a quintessentially American outlook: optimistic, individualistic, anti-institutional, anchored in the belief that we can reinvent ourselves — even the most disadvantaged among us — and overcome the odds, no matter how daunting. It is a perspective that adds up to what might be called the heroic conception of social policy, anchored in the viewpoint that dramatic stories like Sean and John's can be reproduced across America in vast numbers.

These claims are conspicuous not only for their scope and force but for their timing: they arrive at a juncture when education and social policy elsewhere are becoming ever more tentative in their claims and expectations. Even time-honored and research-supported initiatives like Head Start have trouble generating this much passion.

Answering the Call

David Hall, a white man in his forties, is a manager for the city of Milwaukee and a mentor in the One-on-One program. He is matched with Charles, a black junior high school student.

I'm a sixties radical who must have gotten stuck in a time warp: I just have this need to act on my social conscience. I feel very strongly that if I can contribute something — if I can take what I've been given to benefit somebody else, especially a young person who hasn't had the kind of breaks I've had — I feel better about myself and about the community.

Over the years, I have volunteered for a variety of global causes — trying to address homelessness, protesting the war in Vietnam, fighting for civil rights. But with a one-to-one relationship with an individual over an appreciable period of time, the results are much more tangible. Although they're painfully slow in coming.

One tendency in a program like this is to expect to walk in and change a human being's prospects immediately — to be a hero, a role model; to do all kinds of wonderful things, and in short order. If I had gone in with that expectation, I would be extremely disappointed, because it just hasn't happened. It's been as much frustrating as it's been rewarding.

I'm not sure if it's by nature or because he doesn't like me or what the deal is, but my kid is very quiet, he's not given to expressing himself verbally. You go for weeks at a time not knowing how he feels about you personally or about what you're doing, whether he cares, whether you're having any effect at all. By all outward appearances, he appears to be utterly indifferent.

You have to assume there's something useful going on because his absentee rate from school has dropped dramatically over the year and his grade point average has gone up. For the first time in his six or seven years of school, he was on the honor roll. I don't know if that's me, but we spend most of our time working on his homework.

If he's got homework, he's just dying to do it. If he doesn't have homework, he seems to enjoy being read to and I love reading aloud. Occasionally we just converse, though that part is extremely painful—that's the wrong word—it's difficult, because Charles is not emotive, not expressive, at least not with me.

We have done a couple of social things together. I took him to Great America. I have to admit, I hate that place, it's just awful. But I took him after he finished summer school and he seemed to have a nice time—except again he didn't say anything. We went with my son and two other mentors and their students, and he didn't interact with anybody. But he laughed a lot.

Charles is lacking in social graces, in courtesies. He didn't utter a word of thanks for Great America, for Christmas presents. When he got on the honor roll, I was planning to do something special for him. The day of the tutoring session, I told him how proud I was of him and his achievement. Just before he left, he said he wanted a reward. I was so disappointed. I had planned to do something myself, until it became a demand—and I shook his hand and said, "Charles, here is your reward, congratulations, keep up the good work, you ain't near done." Well, I went ahead anyway, put a crisp $10 bill in with a card. Never heard a word.

I don't need him to say thank you to me. What I need him to do is to understand that people do things for other people if they know that their efforts are appreciated. I want him also to know that there are people who care about him. But caring about someone involves give-and-take. It doesn't occur to this child that the fact that someone cares about him is something he ought to appreciate and express his appreciation for. It may be a small thing to him, but it's a big thing to me.

So I talked with him about it and cited every one of these

instances. I ticked them off. And his excuse? "I forgot." I said, "I'm asking you to do these things because they're the right things to do socially, they get you places, people think well of you when you do these things. If that's so easy to forget, then I'll forget about doing [all the things I do for you]." He was silent. He doesn't react, he doesn't react!

Yeah, I take it personally, but what I've learned mostly is that I have to have patience and the willingness to accept Charles's essential character for what it is. He appears to be a quiet kid, maybe because it's hard for sixth- and seventh-graders to relate to people with gray beards who are white; that's very possible. If he wants to talk, sooner or later he'll say something. I've learned to back off and let him take the lead if he wants to. There are certain things I don't compromise on, the goals of the program or the conditions for participating: he's got to stay in school, do his homework, give something of himself in these sessions, just as I do.

I keep going because I believe it's a good thing to do. I care about Charles because he is my charge. He is the human being I have been linked up with and, regardless of what happens, I'll be with him.

3

Recurring
Fervor

The chief need of the poor today is not almsgiving,
but the moral support of true friendship.
—Rev. S. Humphrey Gurteen,
Handbook of Charity Organizations, 1882

*T*he emergence of mentoring, despite so much euphoria, is far from the first appearance of similar ideas on the American stage. The movement's principal elements—middle-class volunteers, a focus on the poor, and reliance on personal relationships— constitute a recurring reform impulse, one responsible for similar fanfare in the past. These earlier episodes reveal a great deal about how Americans often choose to approach social problems and help illuminate the dynamics of the current movement.

Antecedents of Mentoring

While Big Brothers/Big Sisters remains the most familiar antecedent of the current mentoring wave, a still earlier manifestation of this particular reform impulse can be found in the closing decades of the nineteenth century, in a now obscure set of campaigns known as Friendly Visiting.[1]

Friendly Visiting

As the United States entered the final quarter of the nineteenth
century, social relations were badly strained. The great railroad
strike of 1878 was the most violent and wide-ranging labor
conflict in the country's history. Hordes of unemployed men
roamed the country in search of work. Squalid urban slums were
swelling with immigrants, in whose homes one commentator saw
"an immorality as deep as [their] poverty . . . a moral atmosphere
as pestilential as the physical."[2] The country was increasingly
split between the classes of capital and labor; to many, it seemed
to be ripping apart at the seams.

In response to what one reformer called a terrible chasm
between the rich and poor, "a chasm which is becoming wider
and wider as the years roll by," urban civic leaders launched a
new movement of moral and social reform based on the principles of "scientific charity."[3] In cities around the country, charitable societies sprang up, armed with volunteer Friendly Visitors
supported by a few paid agents. These male agents managed
the operation, but the female Friendly Visitors were the main
vessels for carrying out the program.

The Friendly Visiting campaigns were unveiled with extreme optimism and an evangelical fervor. In 1885, one leader,
Charles Kellogg, wrote of a battalion of a hundred thousand
visitors sweeping "like a tidal wave" over urban America, "flood-
ing every part . . . [with] sweetness and order and light."[4]

The immediate objective was moral uplift, "to raise the
character and elevate the moral nature of the poor." The immediate enemy was relief, almsgiving that engendered "habits
of dependence, destroying manliness and self-respect" while making "pauperism a permanent institution, a positive profession."
Almsgiving left the poor person's "heart untouched."[5]

The broader goal was a return to an earlier, organic society in which class tensions were mitigated by bonds of sympathy. According to historian Roy Lubove, whose work *The Professional Altruist* offers the fullest treatment of the movement, Friendly
Visiting sought to "substitute for the spontaneous neighborli-
ness of the small town."[6] In particular, the Friendly Visitors —

like the mentors and the big brothers to follow—were to be role models for children of the poor. As a movement leader, Mary Richmond, explains in her book, *Friendly Visiting Among the Poor,* "We should not despair of the children, so long as we can attach them to us, and give them a new and better outlook upon life."[7]

The vehicle for achieving these goals was an instrumental form of personal relationship, one designed to produce practical results. The visitors were expected "to think of the poor as husbands, wives, sons, and daughters," and to exhibit "all possible sympathy, tact, patience, cheer, and wise advice."[8] As Lubove points out, the tools of the Friendly Visitor were actually a mix of personality and class affiliation; the visitor was "dispatched not as an expert in investigation or the handling of relief, but as the representative of a middle class."[9]

Despite such hopeful beginnings, Friendly Visiting collapsed by the turn of the century. The movement was beset by a profound shortage of volunteer citizens who had enough time to devote to this enterprise. Despite calls for one hundred thousand visitors, the actual numbers were far smaller and trailed off quickly. Increasingly, the functions of the visitors were taken over by the paid agents. In addition, Friendly Visitors found it difficult to help the poor. The genteel and sometimes patronizing outsiders discovered a population more inclined to turn to their friends and neighbors for solace than to the representatives of middle-class life. While a few visitors managed to establish strong personal relationships and be of some help, they were the exception. Finally, the movement was overwhelmed by economic realities. A series of depressions in the late nineteenth century underscored the material basis of poverty and put the power of middle-class friendship in perspective.

Badly battered, Friendly Visiting came to occupy another episode in what historian Paul Boyer describes as a familiar cycle in urban social reform, one proceeding rapidly from "initial enthusiasm to baffled discouragement."[10] By the first years of the twentieth century, even the major elements of Friendly Visiting, middle-class participation in the fight against poverty and an approach based on relationship, had given way to the newly emergent social work profession.

First, the early social workers replaced personal relationship with technical expertise in the form of casework. Next, middle-class volunteers were relegated to ceremonial and ancillary functions in the new social agency bureaucracies, where the real work of dealing with the poor was consolidated in the hands of paid professionals. According to Lubove, what remained was "neither alms nor a friend, but a professional service."[11]

Big Brothers/Big Sisters

Although Lubove's phrase accurately characterizes human service delivery following the demise of Friendly Visiting — and arguably remains true today — the beginning of the new century saw another movement based on middle-class voluntarism and instrumental relationships quietly take form in the shadow of the new bureaucracies.

This new movement was founded by Ernest K. Coulter, a New York newspaperman who left journalism to work in the first children's court in the city. Coulter was appalled at the misery and neglect he witnessed among the youngsters brought before the court, and was concerned that the "justice" the court delivered took little account of their needs and personal problems. He felt this lack was responsible for the high rate of recidivism.

In an address to the Men's Club of the Central Presbyterian Church of New York on December 3, 1904, Coulter shared his perspective with the audience of middle-class businessmen, professionals, and civic leaders. He illustrated his theory with the story of a young boy recently charged with a crime that would likely send him, upon conviction, to a reformatory. Coulter believed the harsh reformatory held little hope for rehabilitation: "There is only one possible way to save that youngster, and that is to have some earnest, true man volunteer to be his big brother, to look after him, help him to do right, make the little chap feel that there is at least one human being in this great city who takes a personal interest in him; who cares whether he lives or dies." In closing, Coulter issued an appeal: "I call for a volunteer."[12] The thirty-nine volunteers who signed up that night became the first Big Brothers.

Their experience was far from easy. Trying to make a home visit, one pioneer Big Brother was greeted by the little brother's mother, wielding a large pistol. Another was menaced with a pan of sudsy dishwater. Coulter himself spent eight years trying to rescue one member of the notorious Fagins street gang. Despite exhaustive efforts, including assistance from other "Bigs" who provided homes, jobs, and support, the boy refused all reformation, eventually disappearing for good.

Despite these initial frustrations, the Big Brothers/Big Sisters movement caught on, soon generating its own fervent supporters. The early euphoria was epitomized by a rally for the new movement held at the Casino Theatre in New York in April 1916. The Casino rally—attended by two thousand men and women, black and white, from all denominations—reflected the strong religious cast of Big Brothers/Big Sisters in its beginning years. The audience was addressed by a series of clergymen who whipped the crowd, according to one historian of the movement, into a "revival-like fervor." The first speaker, a Catholic priest, declared that each adult "must come forward and, man for man and woman for woman, get into this work for the children." The next guest, Rabbi J. L. Magnes, compared wayward youth to "tender plants," declaring: "In this day of cold efficiency—efficiency in business, efficiency in charity—it is a miserable small justice our great organized charities do. . . . The personal touch is absent. It can't be put into a scientific system. . . . It is human."

The final orator, Episcopal Bishop David H. Greer, likened New York to a great storage battery of kindness: "Thousands are ready to do good if they have the opportunity, and this great, happy, growing movement gives them the opportunity." Greer echoed Magnes's concern about the impersonality of existing social bureaucracies, warning: "Not by social machinery are bad boys to be made good boys, but by the warm, personal touch in life."

Alongside concerns about impersonal, arid social welfare bureaucracies and their inability to reach delinquent youth, deeper fears of impending social breakdown propelled the new movement. Big Brothers/Big Sisters grew up as a middle-class movement, part of the broader push of progressivism. Its founders were distressed by the same extremes of wealth and poverty in the United States that had animated the creators of Friendly Visiting. They saw children and youth growing up in poverty as potential sources of social breakdown, in need of socialization, firm guidance and human connection with mainstream adults.

However, unlike Friendly Visiting, which was replaced by professional services in the wake of its inability to live up to unrealistic claims, Big Brothers/Big Sisters managed during the period between the world wars to develop a balance between fervor and operational consistency by a gradual process of professionalizing. In 1921, the first Big Brother/Big Sister Federation was formed, setting standards for programs and one-to-one relationships that aspired to the federation's imprimatur. At first these standards were quite flexible, aiming to cultivate wide acceptance; over time they became firmer and more clearly specified. Eventually the federation evolved into Big Brothers/Big Sisters of America, the body that continues to govern this movement today.

At present, Big Brothers/Big Sisters of America (BB/BSA) consists of 483 local affiliates in forty-one states, matching seventy thousand young people with adult "Bigs." In addition, the program counts forty thousand mostly minority youths on a waiting list. BB/BSA is at present a large, stable, yet still vibrant movement, which owns the rights to the phrase "One-to-One" and enjoys one of the highest levels of name recognition of any organization in America today.

From Mythology to Policy

Just as the earlier interest in voluntarism and relationships was channeled through particular roles—that of the visitor or the big brother and big sister—the current fervor too has its own vessel. The mentor is distinguished from the earlier forms by its status as one of the most enduring and celebrated relationships in our culture. Indeed, mentoring brings with it an entire mythology.

The word *mentor* derives from a Greek tale and, etymologically, from a number of Greek roots meaning "think," "counsel," "remember," and "endure." One contemporary article describes a mentor as a "protector, benefactor, sponsor, champion, advocate, supporter or counselor." Another writer refers to "patrons, guides, and peer pals," while a third adds "host, teacher, and exemplar." The phrase "role model" is frequently invoked.[13]

While these descriptors underscore the complexity of the notion, they only go part of the way toward capturing its essential features. Professor Uri Bronfenbrenner of Cornell University developed a more useful definition following consultation with Japanese scholars about similar relationships in their culture. According to Bronfenbrenner, mentoring is a one-to-one relationship between a pair of unrelated individuals, usually of different ages, and is developmental in nature: "A mentor is an older, more experienced person who seeks to further the development of character and competence in a younger person." Guidance may take many forms, including demonstration, instruction, challenge, and encouragement "on a more or less regular basis over an extended period of time." Furthermore, this relationship is distinguished by "a special bond of mutual commitment" and "an emotional character of respect, loyalty, and identification."[14]

The Classical Conception of Mentoring

Bronfenbrenner's definition distills what might be called the classical conception of mentoring: a robust and highly idealized relationship that has attained mythic proportions in our culture. Stories from several different eras capture its spirit.

Homer's "Mentor." The word *mentor* first appears as a character's name in Homer's *Odyssey* some seven hundred years before the birth of Christ.[15] According to the *Odyssey*, "Mentor was an old friend of Odysseus, to whom the king had entrusted his whole household when he sailed." In particular, the king entrusted to this "wise and faithful friend" the safekeeping and development of his only son, Telemachus.

Mentor attends to this task, but it is only when the goddess Athena, the goddess associated with fortunate adventures, takes on the guise of Mentor that the elevated qualities of the role are revealed. Mentor/Athena tells the young warrior, who is about to embark on the search for his father, "Today has proved you, Telemachus, neither a coward nor a fool. . . . No fear, then, that this journey of yours will end in farce or failure. . . . You have every reason to feel that you will make a success of this undertaking."

Not content merely to impart wisdom and encouragement, Mentor/Athena prepares the way for the boy's important voyage: "You will soon be off on this journey you have set your heart on. For am I not your father's friend, and ready to find you a fast ship and sail with you myself?" After making the promised provisions, the mentor/goddess beckons Telemachus to begin the journey by taking the seat beside him.

The Grimm Brothers' "Iron John." From the 1820s, the Grimm Brothers' story of Iron John, recently revived by the poet Robert Bly, offers another version of the mentoring myth.[16] Iron John is a wild man covered with rust-colored hair. After being captured by the king's hunters, Iron John is caged and displayed in the castle courtyard. The king's young son allows his golden ball to roll into the wild man's cage, and the prisoner offers to return it if the boy will set him free. The youngster retrieves the key, unlocks the gate, and earns Iron John's gratitude. Promising to teach the essentials of life, Iron John carries the boy off on his shoulders.

At this juncture, the wild man becomes the mentor. Assuming the mantle of initiator is a step that Bly compares to the moment in ancient Greek life when a priest of Dionysus accepted a young man as a student, or "the moment in Eskimo life today when the shaman, sometimes covered entirely with the fur of wild animals . . . appears in the village and takes a boy away for spirit instruction."

After imparting the promised life lessons, Iron John compels the boy to leave the forest. Discerning "no evil" in his protégé's heart, he gives the boy a gift: "Whenever you are in trouble, come to the edge of the forest and shout, 'Iron John!' I'll come to the edge of the forest and help you. My power is great, greater than you believe, and I have gold and silver in abundance." Over time, the boy returns on several occasions for Iron John's help. With his mentor's guidance, the boy earns great acclaim as a knight and marries a princess in a neighboring kingdom. At the wedding, the boy is reunited with his parents, as well as with a surprise guest, Iron John. Released from a spell by the boy's achievements, Iron John himself has been transformed back into a king.

Raines's "A Mentor's Presence." A third story, this one from our own time, reveals the continuing vitality of the classical conception of mentoring. In an article in the *New York Times Magazine,* journalist Howell Raines reflects on the influence of his college English professor, Richebourg Gaillard McWilliams.[17] His story, "A Mentor's Presence," reflects many of the same themes we find in earlier tales.

Raines sought and eventually won his professor's affection "to the extent that I came to see myself as something like an honorary son." This relationship was not always easy. McWilliams wanted to harden his students "for the solitary toil of a literary apprenticeship," and he was fond of telling them that "most, if not all, would fail." Indeed, McWilliams predicted that the students who did succeed would not necessarily be the most gifted stylists, but rather those who refused to quit. Then, Raines recalls, the older man would strike "a line across his desk with a thick shiny fingernail," proclaiming, "You must always plow on to the end of the row." Raines adds that the row "stretched for twelve years" between the initial draft and publication of his first novel, which he dedicated to McWilliams. He concludes that the professor "influenced me more than any man I have known other than my own father." According to Raines, that influence included his choice of careers, standards of professional performance, and his sense of personal honor. "In short, he was my mentor, and since his death in February, I have been reflecting on the union of spirit that exists between a mentor and protégé."

Raines defines it thus: "A young man cannot will a relationship with a mentor. It must emerge from the flow of two lives, and it must have the reciprocity of a good romance. The adulation of the younger man must be received with a sheltering affection that, in time, ripens into mature respect between equals. Carried to full term, it is a bond less profound but more complex and subtle than that between father and son, a kinship cemented by choice rather than biology." For Raines, "There will be no one else like Richebourg McWilliams in my life, nor would I want there to be."

The Common Elements

As Raines's words attest, the myth of mentoring is enormously sympathetic, and the mentors portrayed in the preceding stories are heroic figures. All three are endowed with great wisdom. There is even the suggestion of the supernatural in two of these tales — Mentor is a goddess in disguise; Iron John's powers are great, "greater than you believe." The magic of mentors, like their wisdom, is applied particularly to aid their protégés' "journey."

As they glorify the mentoring relationship, these tales reveal a trio of elements at the very heart of the classical conception of mentoring: *achievement, nurturance,* and *generativity.*

Achievement. Homer's Mentor prepares the way for Telemachus's journey, providing the necessary equipment, encouraging him, even volunteering to accompany him on his search. Iron John promises to provide his young prince with help along the way in his life's journey. Professor McWilliams teaches Howell Raines how to be competent at his chosen vocation; he warns him against being excessively "mawkish," instructs him to work hard, and remains a sympathetic critic long after Raines graduates from college. With their mentors' help, all three protégés succeed in their trying journeys: Telemachus finds his father, the young prince becomes a successful knight, and Raines develops into a published novelist and established writer. Befitting the genre, all the stories progress to happy endings.

Nurturance. Equally important, the mentors contribute to another journey, conducting their protégés into adulthood. As psychologist Daniel Levinson points out, the mentor functions as a "transitional figure who invites and welcomes a young man into the adult world.[18] Part of this transition is accomplished through the provision of "life lessons," as Iron John promises the young prince. They are lessons in character, to wit: Raines attributes not only his choice of career and professional standards to McWilliams, but his sense of "personal honor."

These lessons take place within the context of a nurturing relationship. Robert Bly describes mentors as "male mothers" interested in "nurturing souls."[19] Howell Raines describes a relationship characterized by "sheltering affection," one with the "reciprocity of a good romance."

Generativity. Finally, mentoring relationships are intergenerational, characterized by the voluntary assumption of responsibility for members of the next generation. They are an expression of what Erik Erikson calls generativity, the impulse to pass on values, culture, and lifeblood to the next generation. In Erikson's view, generativity constitutes the hallmark of successful midlife development, and the mentors in these tales all demonstrate this impulse.[20] In the process, they gain themselves: for example, Iron John is freed from his hex, and McWilliams reaps the satisfaction of having shaped a good writer and contributed to the ongoing vitality of letters.

Traditional mentoring stories, based on the classical conception, concern themselves almost exclusively with men and boys. In fact, it is difficult to locate mentoring stories involving women and girls. To this day, the classical conception of mentoring continues to enjoy broad currency in the sphere of male adult development, as evidenced by such works as Levinson's *Seasons of a Man's Life* and Bly's *Iron John*. Over the past decade, however, mentoring has become more closely associated with women in at least one sphere: career development, particularly in the corporate world.

Moving Up: Mentoring Goes Corporate

While the classical conception of mentoring continues to be prominent, a second incarnation gained force in the 1970s. This variation of the original concept emphasizes mentoring's instrumental aspects, those fostering achievement, over its more nurturing and generative dimensions. One early 1980s reviewer, Sharan Merriam, commented on the fervor this form of mentoring had engendered: "The subject of talk shows, business seminars, journal and magazine articles, the interest in mentoring has reached . . . 'mania' proportions. The listener or reader is told that mentoring is the key to career and academic success." She concludes: "Women in particular are being advised to find one and be one to another woman."

As the previous section suggests, achievement and mentoring have long been associated. Indeed, as Merriam states, "History is replete with examples of such relationships: Socrates and Plato, Freud and Jung, Lorenzo de' Medici and Michelangelo, Haydn and Beethoven, Boas and Mead, Sartre and de Beauvoir, and so on."[21] Retrospective research studies, too, have often focused on such a connection, ranging from a 1926 study, "The Early Mental Traits of Three Hundred Geniuses," which portrays mentoring as important in the lives of many of its subjects, to a more recent review of Nobel laureates in the sciences, which finds a similar tie.[22] However, nowhere has this reduction of the broader notion of mentoring to a highly instrumental one been more thorough than in the corporate world. One reviewer comments that in opposition "to the classical notion of a young person being guided in all aspects of life by an older, wiser person . . . the business world sees it as a one-dimensional phenomenon in which the protégé's career is guided by a senior organization person."[23]

In fact, researchers and observers have recently focused on the critical role of mentoring as a cornerstone of the "old boy network." A 1978 *Harvard Business Review* article described and glorified the role in profiling three male executives. Its title's message, "everyone who makes it has a mentor,"[24] has been echoed in scores of other stories in the business press. It is no accident that these articles began appearing at the time when more and more women were entering management ranks, confronting the "glass ceiling," and discovering the power of the old boy network.

Many of these women were casting about for ways to ascend the ladder of mobility; for some, the search led to mentoring.

However, women's search for mentors has often proved difficult. In *Men and Women of the Corporation,* Rosabeth Kanter concluded that "the number of mentoring relationships available to women does not appear to be keeping pace with the increasing number of women needing mentors." She found that most mentors in the corporations she studied were male: most managers were male and preferred to mentor aspirants like themselves. Arguing that mentors make a difference in the prospects of their protégés — by going to battle for them, providing help in circumventing bureaucratic roadblocks, and casting reflected power — Kanter advocated "artificial sponsorship programs" for women and minorities, who inevitably found upward mobility blocked. In a later study of another corporation, Kanter argued that women who didn't make it failed due to the absence of mentors, among other supports.[25]

Many subsequent works echoed Kanter's perspective. In *The Corporate Connection: Why Executive Women Need Mentors to Reach the Top,* Agnes Missirian reported the results of a survey of one hundred top businesswomen and argued that mentoring was an important element in their achievement.[26] In *The Managerial Woman,* Hennig and Jardim studied twenty-five women executives and found that every one had a mentor. This discovery led them to advocate that women in corporations "look for a coach, a godfather or a godmother, a mentor, an advocate, someone in a more senior position who can teach . . . support . . . advise . . . critique."[27]

Not surprisingly, women's quest for mentors moved quickly from research to action, spawning an entire industry of how-to books and seminars. A good example is the 1982 book, *Mentors and Protégés: How to Establish, Strengthen and Get the Most from a Mentor/Protégé Relationship.*[28] Corporate seminar companies like Career Track began offering sessions specifically designed to teach these skills.

In its translation from a classical notion to the corporate world, mentoring became increasingly defined not only as *in-*

strumental, a strategy for success, but as *intentional,* something that could be engineered. With the seminars, how-to manuals, and other self-help tools came a wave of mentoring programs for women and minorities, both traditionally cut off from paths to success in large commercial institutions. Along the way, these programs spread to other areas of endeavor, most notably education.

Answering the Call

Sandy Lawrence is vice president of a national investment banking firm. A single white woman in her early forties, she is mentor to Teri, a black high school student in the Cleveland Career Beginnings program.

I've done a lot of volunteer work and work with nonprofits, like sitting on boards, but wasn't getting the right satisfaction out of it. I wanted to try a one-on-one situation.

But there's another side to this for me. I was the first one in my family to go to college, and it took a lot of people helping me in a lot of different ways—in terms of support and encouragement and guidance —for me to make it. For the people who did help me, this is sort of my way of putting back. So when I saw this program, I just jumped at the chance. And it's put another dimension in my life.

Teri is a very talented athlete, a bright and personable human being. She has a lot of things going for her. She is the star volleyball player in the city, MVP two years in a row. The first time I met her she talked about the volleyball team. She went through each person on the team, their strengths and weaknesses, what motivates them. I was so impressed, a sixteen-year-old able to do that. We need to develop young people with this quality of leadership and give them all the help they can get.

Teri's also had a lot to overcome—in particular, her whole family situation. The week before the SATs, her mother moved out of their apartment and sent her to her grandmother's. So the SATs didn't come out to what they should have. But it goes deeper. Her mother's boyfriend moved in the day after her father was killed, and the murder was unsolved. She and her brother think the boyfriend had something to do with it. So she doesn't feel she can talk about the loss of her father to her mother. And when you try to figure out where Teri came from, there must have been something special about her father, that she got before he was gone, and that she's been able to carry on with.

Sometimes we can't figure out where Teri came from, but there are other kids like her in the mentor program, who, despite everything, are survivors. They are bright to begin with, and they've managed to teach themselves a lot. There is something special about them.

Teri's track coach and I work closely together. Our objective is to get Teri out of here to college, far away to college. We had her send applications to top colleges. The University of Arizona was very interested in her, so I got my company to pay for the ticket there. They offered her a scholarship and she has signed a letter of intent with them.

When I was taking her to the airport, she was bewildered about how this was happening and she said, "Why would somebody do this for me?" And I said, "Because they want to help you succeed, because you have a lot of potential and we want to make sure you have the opportunities." And she said, "But they don't even know me." She was shaking her head about this, and when I dropped her off she said, "I hope someday I'll be able to do something like this for somebody."

It's not as hard for us to bridge socioeconomic gaps as I understand it is for other mentor/mentees, but it's still hard, even after two years. There's probably a lot I will never be able to understand about her life, but there's also a lot that she still prefers to keep from me. Partly I think it's her sense of sparing me, partly it's embarrassment. But there are a lot of parallels in our lives, which I think astonishes her, and it's helped bridge the gap. My parents were divorced when I was young, her father was murdered when she was ten. We've both faced these kinds of losses, and when my father died about a month ago I talked to her about it, and it brought up a lot of feelings about her own father's death.

I think mentoring is so important. With all the other efforts *we make with youth and education, it all comes back to one-on-one. We act like we're discovering something new, but when you look back at American life, it used to be broken down on a much smaller scale. There was a lot of interaction between young people and adults in the community. Now there's so much mobility, so much fragmentation, people don't even know their next-door neighbors.*

In a sense I'm disenchanted with the social program system. A lot of "people-to-people" programs and things that folks in the community got involved in providing themselves in the sixties have almost completely disappeared. Simple things like drop-in centers. We don't have them and the kids don't have anywhere else to go. How can we say the kids shouldn't be out on the street, and do absolutely nothing to provide anywhere else for them to go? One of my biggest surprises is the yearning of these kids. A lot of Teri's friends would like to have mentors, would like to have this opportunity. They are into drugs because they want, and they just can't see anything else.

But you know, any mentoring program is just a match service. And it can end up really being worse than having no mentors at all, because if people aren't prepared, they drop out. And Teri has told me about her friends at school in the program. One has a mentor that she's never met, who just calls her on the phone. How can you possibly have a relationship like that, and what does that tell the student? That she's not good enough or important enough for that person to even take the trouble to meet her. Then there's another friend. Her mentor just dropped out in the middle, no closure, noth-ing. That's worse than no mentor at all, because you raised expec-tations, then dashed them again. For these children, it's betrayal of trust all over again.

4

Birth of
a Movement

Millions of kids across the country are starving, but they're not hungry for a balanced meal. They're starved for adult attention.
— One PLUS One,
A Special Report on Mentoring

*I*f the classical conception of mentoring was the first wave of the notion and the corporate incarnation was the second, then the late 1980s ushered in what amounts to the third. Like its immediate predecessor, this third wave is characterized by instrumental and intentional tendencies and by the use of volunteers drawn from the professional class. The significant difference is the target group: disadvantaged children and youth.

The third wave of mentoring brings with it an obvious question: Why has mentoring become so popular at this time as a vehicle for ameliorating the needs of young people in poverty? As the movement's diversity and decentralized character suggest, its emergence can be traced to a number of factors: the dire circumstances of disadvantaged youth, the yearning and frustration felt by many middle-class adults, the current crisis in education and social policy, and mentoring's inherent qualities as a mechanism, so evident in its long history.

42

Youth Adrift

In explaining their objectives, mentoring's proponents cite the growing isolation of young people from caring adult contact. One PLUS One, the Public Broadcasting System's project to stimulate mentoring, stresses the urgency of millions of kids starving for adult attention. In her SOS, Dorothy Gilliam invokes the predicament of youth in isolated neighborhoods, cut off from decent adult role models. This absence of attention and models is portrayed as stunting youth academically, vocationally, and developmentally, while contributing more broadly to social breakdown.

The comments by One PLUS One and Dorothy Gilliam offer two different but interrelated arguments for mentoring. The first is a characterization of young people living in personal isolation, yearning for adult attention; the second is a tale of moral isolation, of youth growing up bereft of pro-social influences, cut off from the mainstream society. While both images are oversimplifications, and *isolation* amounts much more to a code word than a precise description of the condition of inner-city youth, each depiction contains important truths identified by researchers of adolescents as real and pressing problems.

Growing Up Alone

Widespread family breakdown, the erosion of many neighborhood ties, and the time demands of work—for adults and for many youth—have driven a wedge between the generations. The Carnegie Council for Adolescent Development asserts, "Many young people feel a desperate sense of isolation," a condition that frequently results in "poor decisions with harmful or lethal consequences."[1] Psychologist Laurence Steinberg observes that "few young people in America today have even one significant, close relationship with a non-familial adult before reaching adulthood themselves."[2] He adds that this is a far different state of affairs than in the past.

Sociologist James Coleman of the University of Chicago

conceptualizes the problem in terms of a decline in the "social capital" available to youth. For Coleman, social capital is different from human capital, which is located in knowledge or skills. Social capital derives from "the norms, the social networks, and the relationships between adults and children that are of value for the child's growing up."[3]

As households shrink and parents work longer hours, social capital dries up in the home. Outside the home, it can be absorbed in the community through the interest, even the intrusiveness, of adults in the activities of neighborhood children, ranging from lending a sympathetic ear to enforcing community norms. However, here too, Coleman finds social capital in decline, stating that "in the individualistic present, each narcissistically attends to self-development, with little attention left over for children, certainly not for others' children." He goes on to argue, based on a series of studies of public and parochial schools, that the absence of social capital adversely affects school performance.

While expressing concern about the deterioration of adult-youth relationships across the socioeconomic spectrum, Coleman and others contend that this erosion is particularly damaging to young people living in poverty. One reason is that more affluent families can compensate to some degree by spending money, through paying for adult interaction for their kids in the form of after-school programs, summer camp, even counseling and therapy. As a result, young people in poverty often have considerably less adult support to draw on than their middle-class contemporaries. The 1988 National Educational Longitudinal Study indicates, for example, that youth in the lowest socioeconomic group are most likely to be home alone and unsupervised for three or more hours after school.[4]

However, merely to count the hours in the presence of adults does little to flesh out the concept of isolation. Rather, this notion must be understood in context, against the backdrop of stress confronting young people growing up in disadvantaged urban neighborhoods.

By the age of fifteen, 30 percent of young people living in our inner cities have witnessed a killing, while 70 percent have seen someone beaten. These experiences have led researchers to compare American urban environments with those in war zones like Beirut and Belfast; these studies reveal a common state of lost childhood among youth in such zones, a condition forcing these young people to shut down emotionally or assume an aggressive bravado. James Garbarino of the Erikson Institute suggests that circumstances in the United States are actually worse than those in even the most violence-ridden situations abroad: "At least in a war zone you know the battle will end and peace may come. But with community violence in America the war never ends and peace never comes."[5]

These traumatizing experiences, while creating additional need for support, simultaneously make it more difficult for many disadvantaged youth to accept or attract the assistance they need. At the same time, poverty works in multiple and reinforcing ways to cut off sources of potential help.

The deindustrialization of the urban economy compromises the job prospects of low-income males, thereby lowering their financial capacity to support a family and reducing the likelihood of two-parent households.[6] Furthermore, conditions surrounding poverty, most notably the use of crack cocaine, contribute to the incidence of "no parent" households — which grew by 50 percent from 1970 to 1990 — as more and more women succumb to the devastation of drugs and as grandparents, relatives, and institutions are pressed into raising children.[7]

Finally, the violence and stress of inner-city life traumatizes not only children but their adult caregivers, substantially reducing their capacity to nurture others; research shows that in particularly hard-hit urban neighborhoods as many as half the mothers are suffering from severe depression. These circumstances are further exacerbated by high levels of domestic violence mirroring the surrounding neighborhood violence.[8]

The combination of high stress and inadequate social support means that a great many young people today can count on few buffers against daily trauma. They are emotionally and psychologically imperiled, not only "cheated of childhood," but very often robbed of the opportunity to develop into emotionally healthy adults.

Growing Up Alienated

An accumulation of evidence suggests that children in poverty are suffering from a second, equally severe form of isolation — one social in nature. Sociologist William Julius Wilson and others researching inner-city neighborhoods warn that impoverished youth no longer have access to the range of mainstream adults who served as role models and socializers of preceding generations. According to Wilson, these figures "helped keep alive the perception that education is meaningful, that steady employment is a viable alternative to welfare, and that family stability is the norm, not the exception."[9]

In explaining this change, Wilson stresses demographics, contending these middle-class models no longer play an important part in community life because they no longer live in the community, having departed the urban ghettos in droves following progress on fair housing. He marshalls evidence showing that inner-city neighborhoods today are both poorer and more economically homogeneous than in the past.

Without contesting that the departure of middle-class blacks weakened the fabric of the inner city and the social capital available to its young people, ethnographers studying these neighborhoods offer a much fuller picture of what has happened at the grassroots level. In particular, they show that explanations rooted in exodus of the wealthier classes are only part of the story. Many lower-income role models, individuals embodying the same values and behaviors Wilson upholds in the black middle class, remain in inner-city communities; however, their availability, status, and influence are in sharp decline.

Elijah Anderson of the University of Pennsylvania calls these figures "old heads," and in *Streetwise,* his study of the inner-city Philadelphia neighborhood he calls Northton, Anderson describes the old head/youth relationship as "essentially one of mentor and protégé."[10]

For generations, the old head was an essential aspect of the social fabric of Northton and was critical to the stability of traditional black communities like it. In the case of males, the old head might be a minister or deacon in the church, policeman, coach, or street-corner man. Regardless of title, the old head's acknowledged role was "to teach, support, encourage, and in effect socialize young men to meet their responsibilities with regard to the work ethic, family life, the law, and decency." These individuals, furthermore, served as bridges to the world outside the neighborhood, particularly in the area of employment. They not only urged young boys to "get a trade," but provided contacts leading to employment in blue-collar jobs.

Although Anderson concentrates on males, he also describes the traditional functions of female old heads, who served "an important fictive kinship role of extra parent or surrogate mother" and were integral in providing informal support, discipline, and social sanction. According to one such woman: "The way I feel about it, the way I tell these children is, 'I love all children; if you don't love somebody else['s] children, you don't love [your] own.'"

Based on his study of Northton, Anderson argues that the position of the old head is greatly weakened in urban neighborhoods today. In part, this is due to the erosion of the values they embody — of responsibility, restraint, deferred gratification — in the larger American culture. In the immediate environment, the old head's salience is undercut by the loss of meaningful employment in the inner cities. Their teachings carry far less weight and make less intuitive sense in the context of little opportunity, as the means through which they established themselves is no longer visible or available to the next generation.

The growing violence of inner-city neighborhoods further leads to the decline of the role of old head, through its contribution to the deterioration of public trust and public interaction. Old heads, male and female, conducted their socialization functions in public; however, "as the community has experienced the coming and going of so many residents, social life has become less stable." Worst of all, with the rise of drugs, crime, and violence, "residents feel especially distant and wary around strangers. Public spaces have become increasingly complicated and dangerous, or at least they are perceived that way." In this changing context, many old heads have ceased to participate in the community, and in fact they are mocked by neighborhood youth "who patronize the old heads . . . for not understanding 'the way the world really works.'"

In *Slim's Table,* ethnographer Mitchell Duneier adds to Anderson's portrait by describing a group of black, mostly lower-income men living in an urban ghetto on Chicago's south side. These individuals share a deep commitment to the ethos of respectability, responsibility, and decency, but are essentially living in exile within their own communities. Although they still live in the ghetto, they have been forced to find a separate location where they can feel comfortable and engage in the kind of social interaction that used to occur in public.[11]

Duneier studies one such world, a nearby restaurant, Valois's "See Your Food" Cafeteria. For these men Valois's is a refuge from the social disorganization prevalent in their neighborhood. As one explains, "I'll tell you why everyone comes down to Valois's. It is to escape from the realities of dealing with people outside of the cafeteria. Here it's like a separate world." Like Anderson, Duneier describes the intense "moral isolation" of these formerly central figures in the socialization process and their profound alienation from the current generation of black youth.

The exodus and the exile of the old heads corresponds with the ascendance of a new group of models and mentors, the drug dealers and gang leaders whom Dorothy Gilliam laments. These new models are consummate "individualist survivors," tireless entrepreneurs who work a 24/7 — twenty-four hours a day, seven days a week — in pursuit of the American Dream. While their wares only serve to destroy lives and the community, the dealers are nonetheless compelling figures in a wider culture that idealizes fast wealth, conspicuous consumption, and the self-made man, in a local environment where few conventional opportunities to make it are available.

The Collapse of Neighborhood

The composite that emerges from this picture of interpersonal and social isolation goes beyond the replacement of one role with another. It adds up to the collapse of what psychiatrist James Comer of Yale Medical School calls the "developmental infra-

structure" of poor neighborhoods, an interlocking set of relationships that helped protect and nurture young people in the
past.[12] Comer recalls growing up in a low-income black neighborhood near Chicago where "between home and school, at least
five friends of my parents reported everything I did that was
unacceptable," observing that this network is "not there anymore
for today's kids." In Comer's neighborhoods not only was there
considerable interaction between adults and youth, but among
a variety of related and unrelated adults who had a stake in the
young person's life — parents, teachers, ministers, coaches, and
others. The result was a tightly linked web of support, one infused with natural mentoring and built around the notion of
fictive kinship.

What happens in the absence of this community? One consequence is that it becomes much more difficult for young people to survive emotionally, grow developmentally, and establish
linkages to the outside society. Philosopher Cornel West of Princeton sees the damage going even deeper. For West, the shatter-
ing of black civil society provides an opening for the threat of
nihilism, a threat that has always faced Americans living in
poverty, kept at bay in the past by roles like the old head and
institutions such as the church.[13]

By nihilism, West does not mean some arcane philosophi-
cal doctrine but rather "the lived experience of coping with a
life of horrifying meaninglessness, hopelessness, and (most important) lovelessness," adding that life without meaning, hope,
and love breeds a "coldhearted, mean-spirited outlook that de-
stroys both the individuals and others." This assertion is supported not only by the astronomical rise in inner-city homicides
over the past decade, but by other indications as well: until the
early 1970s, for example, black Americans had the lowest sui-
cide rate of any group in the United States; today young blacks
lead the country in this category of despair.

A Powerful Impulse

Despite the terrible realities of youth isolation, it would be a mistake to attribute the rise of mentoring exclusively to the cry of
unmet urban needs. Equally important to mentoring's emergence

are cultural and social currents circulating through the lives of middle-class adults.

Even growing awareness of the isolation of poor kids can be traced as much to the circumstances of mainstream adults as to those of these disadvantaged youth. In recent years, we have seen a universalization of the conditions of poverty, as middle-class parents are increasingly forced to raise children while working. They, too, must cope with stress and the loss of adequate social support. The difficulty these families encounter in spending time with their own children makes more believable the isolation of poor children and more compelling the warnings about its deleterious effects. As this example suggests, there are many parallels, at the interpersonal and social levels, between the plight of poor children and the conditions confronting mainstream adults in our society.

To Make a Difference

American historian and social commentator Arthur Schlesinger notes the existence of "a lot of pent-up idealism" and has predicted another round in America's cyclical response to poverty, arguing that "in the 1990s we'll enter a phase that will be like the 1930s and 1960s."[14] In rare agreement with the liberal Schlesinger, William F. Buckley also detects a population eager to express a "civic sense of obligation."[15]

Supporting both Schlesinger and Buckley are a number of recent polls, including a Gallup survey commissioned by the nonprofit group Independent Sector, which found growing interest in voluntarism and charitable giving, particularly among adults of the "baby boom" generation. As the director of the Independent Sector study suggests, "These influences add up to more charitable giving and more volunteering for community service."[16]

Mentors reflect this persistent idealism, an idealism shaped during the 1960s and early 1970s, and express frustration over professional situations limiting opportunities to act on social conscience. Echoing Schlesinger, Sandy Lawrence observes a cycle underway in the society, led by baby boomers "who went through a lot of stuff in the sixties, had their idealism dented, and decided it's not so easy to pursue these ideals and make the mortgage payment." However, these individuals continue "to wrestle with what we want versus what should be." Her own response is to attempt both: to earn her professional salary in real-estate development while "trying to broaden opportunities for other people."

Like Lawrence, Washington, D.C. mentor Gerald Green moved from the public to private sectors during the 1980s. He was formerly in VISTA, then legal services, then the federal government. Now, as partner in a large law firm, he admits, "It's a little hard to believe you're doing much for society." Green describes mentoring as a vehicle for reincorporating a service element in his life. He adds another reason—that of community: "What's going on is a lot of people seeking types of service opportunities that would get them involved in some sense of community—whether it's working with the homeless, working on AIDS issues, or doing some sort of mentoring." David Hall explains that mentoring not only makes him feel better about himself but about the community.

Many African-American mentors particularly emphasize the importance of community in their decision to come forward. Ben Warren describes the decision to mentor "as a way of reaching back to the neighborhood," specifically to the inner-city Philadelphia neighborhood where he grew up. He describes a very personal sense of responsibility, explaining, "If I can help one guy make something out of himself, that's one less guy I think has potential of *not* making something out of himself. If I didn't do it and I had the opportunity to do it, I would feel bad."

Derek Sutton, an African-American corporate executive with MCI, was initially resistant when asked to mentor: "I said, 'I've got enough on my plate already. I have a son of my own I'm trying to get into college.' I asked myself, with all the things I'm asked to do in the company, why add another piece?" His decision to come forward, despite so many other commitments, was based on a simple question he could not answer: "If I'm not going to do this—feel this is imperative—then who else is?"

The current revival of responsibility among mentors black

and white — the impulse often described as the desire to make a difference — can also be seen as a reaction to the excesses and inequalities of the 1980s: the vast gulfs that opened up between rich and poor (and between rich and middle-class) and the visible consequences of cutbacks in government spending on social services. These societal changes all contribute to a reaction similar to that which animated Friendly Visiting and the Big Brothers/ Big Sisters movements in earlier times.

Somewhat ironically in this context, a select group of millionaires' assuming responsibility for classes of poor children around the country became an important catalyst in the formation of the mentoring movement. Eugene Lang, first and most influential, widely dramatized the practice and promise of taking responsibility for poor children. Through his "I Have a Dream" project, he helped to create a sense of hope at a moment during the 1980s when hope was in short supply. Lang, a self-made millionaire, returned to his East Harlem elementary school, half a century after he had left, to deliver the commencement address. He ended up issuing a spontaneous promise to the graduating class of sixth-graders: to pay for their college educations if they completed high school and gained admission to college.

Lang's initiative is now familiar, not only as the subject of extensive media coverage but also as the impetus for hundreds of millionaires around the country to reproduce this project and variations on it. Financier Ray Chambers, founder of One to One and co-chair of the Points of Light Foundation, is among the individuals who attribute their current activism to Lang. It is not surprising that in the midst of the 1980s — a decade that glorified wealth and the wealthy — a set of millionaires should be cast in the role of social action heroes. However, Lang used the limelight not only to encourage the assumption of personal responsibility and to dramatize the prospect of helping young people in poverty but also to emphasize that the key ingredient to his project's success was getting personally involved in a mentor-like role with young people. In fact, he argues today that the scholarship offer for which I Have a Dream is most famous is a "vestigial" part of the program: its real significance lies in emphasizing continuity of caring over a six-year period as well as concentration of caring, through providing an array of adults with an interest in the young person's life.

I Have a Dream has contributed to the rise of mentoring in another way as well. In the midst of all its celebrity, this effort has generated a set of tough questions: how many millionaires are ultimately ready to do what Lang has done, year in and year out? What about the kids not lucky enough to have a millionaire benefactor? What might the average person do to help?

Many organizations, corporations, and cities have responded to these questions by "democratizing the Dream," by creating mentoring programs where individuals interested in helping — but without the means to adopt an entire class of students — could take responsibility for a single youth. Indeed many of the most prominent mentoring efforts around the country, such as Milwaukee's One-on-One and Project RAISE in Baltimore, began as attempts to reproduce the I Have a Dream project.

To Make a Connection

The desire to make a difference, described by so many mentors and by those initiating programs, is only one of the impulses behind this movement. There is a parallel one — to make a connection, to reach out in a personal, direct, and immediate way.

In the mid-nineteenth century, Alexis de Tocqueville commented that American life tends to isolate citizens within the solitude of their own hearts.[17] In interviews with contemporary middle-class adults (individuals in many respects similar to the group that has come forward to mentor) sociologist Robert Bellah and a group of colleagues have located a middle-class population locked in similar solitude and experiencing a deeply felt yearning for connection. Their observations are confirmed by a recent J. Walter Thompson survey revealing that almost three out of four Americans do not even know the people living next door.[18] In *Habits of the Heart,* Bellah and his colleagues found, "Few of those with whom we talked have found a life devoted to 'personal ambition and consumerism' satisfactory, and most are seeking in one way or another to transcend the limitations of a self-centered life." In particular, they conclude, "There is in the desire for intense relationships with others an attempt to move beyond the isolated self."[19]

A range of investigators support Bellah in identifying this yearning for connection. Psychologists interested in adult development find a growing need for Erikson's notion of *generativity,* the "instinctual drive to create and care for new life," essentially taking care to "pass on to the next generation what you've contributed to life."[20]

Erikson's notion contains two facets, one deriving from the Greek word *caritas,* which he defines broadly as a sense of caring for others, the second emanating from *agape,* which the psychoanalyst interprets as a kind of empathy. These impulses come together in the developmentally successful adult in an appreciation of human interdependence, most fully expressed in concern about posterity. The final crisis of life, Erikson argues, is marked by coming to terms with the notion, "I am what survives of me." Reflecting on the state of contemporary American life, Erikson believes we are in the midst of a widespread and debilitating crisis, arguing that "the only thing that can save us as a species is seeing how we're not thinking about future generations in the way we live." For the psychoanalyst, "What's lacking is . . . a generativity that will promote positive values in the lives of the next generation."

Inherent in the perspectives of Erikson, Bellah, and others is the idea that adults in our society are, in some ways, just as "at-risk" as youth. Just as the younger generation is impoverished through isolation from adults, the development of adults is frustrated by their tenuous ties with the young. The developmental infrastructure that we've lost carried with it opportunities for meeting the emotional needs of both generations. It is not surprising that focus groups among "baby boomers," for example, locate a strong preference for voluntarism involving direct contact and personal relationships.[21] Mentoring appears to draw on and reflect this yearning to help in an immediate and very personal way, and mentors interviewed expressed the desire to build more contact with youth into personal and professional lives permitting few natural opportunities for this kind of connection.

An Appealing Vessel

Contributing to mentoring's rise, along with the circumstances of youth and adults in our society, is the current crisis in education and social policy. At the same time that natural roles and traditions supporting youth are breaking down, the public institutions that might compensate, most notably schools, are failing to do so. These institutions are more often than not, in the words of former U.S. Commissioner of Education Harold Howe II, "impersonal teaching factories," places where individuals are, according to another observer, "melting into ciphers." Educational reform efforts emphasizing testing and standards have done little to dispel this perception and have likely worsened the reality.[22]

The funding cutbacks of the Reagan and Bush years, coupled with the flight of middle-class families from urban centers, means that public schools have been forced to offer large classes while cutting back activities that make adult-youth contact possible. One telling instance of this crisis is the status of guidance counselors. In New York, for example, there are 2,000 guidance counselors for 930,000 students. An average elementary school counselor maintains a caseload of 750 students, all the while confronting needs on the part of students far exceeding those in the past. There are simply too few counselors — indeed, too few adults — in schools to do much to handle the daily crises in youths' lives, much less compensate for missing social capital.[23]

The crisis is not confined to the schools, as a recent Carnegie Council on Adolescent Development task force on the state of community youth organizations concludes. *A Matter of Time: Risk and Opportunity in the Non-School Hours* charts the dearth of youth organizations in many urban neighborhoods and the failure of large national youth-serving organizations to meet the needs of disadvantaged young people. The report stresses the critical importance of adult relationships for the development of early adolescence, but finds that "many programs experience high staff turnover because of low salaries and inattention to staff development," adding that "insufficient funding within the sector . . . contributes to lack of dependability in staff and volunteer relationships with youth."[24]

The inability of institutions such as schools and community youth programs to compensate for the collapse of the developmental infrastructure in the lives of poor children contributes to a frantic search for new responses and mechanisms, fueled during the 1980s by government withdrawal from so much of social policy. In the context of this crisis in social policy and education, mentoring has emerged as an appealing vehicle to address both the isolation of youth from adult contact and the incompleteness that many middle-class adults find in their own lives. In the words of one practitioner, it offers a way to tap "a very, very live spirit in association with a recognized need."

And mentoring comes amid a shortage of such vehicles for matching spirit and need. Indeed, as Nicholas Lemann remarks, despite growing sentiment in favor of "reestablishing the social linkages" between the poor and the rest of society, there are few avenues to make the connection.[25] The avenue of mentoring brings with it a set of timely and attractive properties that helps explain its emergence as a means of achieving social linkage.

First, mentoring is *simple*. The "one to one" concept takes an overwhelming set of social problems, such as those associated with poverty, and makes them comprehensible by focusing on the needs of a single youngster. One group states, "Maybe you can't change the world, but you can make a difference in the future of at least one young person."[26] In this way, mentoring personalizes responsibility and allows the individual to act. As another mentoring program tells prospective volunteers, "There is at least one teenager in this city who may not make it to college . . . without you."[27]

Second, mentoring is *direct*. Mentoring simultaneously satisfies a sense of urgency and a desire to cut through red tape to help youth directly. It doesn't require faith in intermediary institutions. It enables individuals to draw on their own resources, as an article about the volunteers in the Princeton 55 mentoring program states: "They didn't want to become another grant-making organization. They decided instead to develop programs that would make the most of their class's time and expertise."[28]

Third, mentoring is highly *sympathetic*. Being dubbed a

mentor is neither neutral nor objective, like tutor or volunteer. It is an honor that flatters the volunteer. As we have seen, mentoring taps into a venerable mythology in our culture that is invariably portrayed in a positive light. The positive perception of mentors has been further boosted by the renaissance that the mentoring notion has enjoyed in popular culture and the corporate world. Indeed, Robert Bly's message that modern men need more mentors has made *Iron John* into a bestseller and has led to a round of backwoods retreats that have drawn an estimated fifty thousand men nationwide.

Fourth, mentoring is *legitimate*. It is a sanctioned role for unrelated adults to play in the lives of youth, as reflected by the many stories that help maintain its respected place in our culture. Big Brothers/Big Sisters helped give it additional legitimacy as a role that could be engineered through social programs. This group maintains one of the highest levels of name recognition of any organization in America and boasts a list of honorary chairs that includes presidents and dignitaries stretching back to Theodore Roosevelt. Without Big Brothers/Big Sisters' long-standing work in bringing together unrelated adults and children in private, personal, one-to-one relationships, it is hard to imagine that a mentoring movement could ever have been launched. Concerns about infringing on parents' prerogatives and about potential abuse would simply have been too formidable.

Fifth, mentoring is *bounded*. One mentor states, "I have a strong interest in kids. But I am not interested in being a mother and I like the mentoring role because it allows me what I consider the appropriate amount of contact with children." Another says that mentoring allows him to be both close and at a distance, adding that while he feels a strong tie with his mentee when they're together, "when he's not around, he's not around." This mentor describes the experience as being like the "best parts of parenting without the worst parts." Both of these mentors are talking about what Princeton University sociologist Robert Wuthnow calls bounded love.[29] Mentoring suggests emotional limits — it is not the same as asking someone to be a parent or to adopt a child. The concept of bounded love makes it easier for potential mentors to come forward without fear of being logistically and emotionally overwhelmed; it also makes it easier to involve unrelated adults without threatening parents.

Finally, mentoring is *plastic,* accommodating whatever attributes people want to give it. Nearly everyone can find something to like in mentoring. At one level, it speaks to the American traditions of individual achievement, progress, and optimism. It is connected to the possibility of an improved work force and economic competitiveness, what one observer terms "kids as capital." At the same time, mentoring has another, more subtle allure. This aspect speaks to the yearning for community lost, to a time of greater civility and responsibility for strangers.

All these factors combine to explain why mentoring has drawn such a diverse group of proponents — encompassing liberals and conservatives, blacks and whites, Republicans and Democrats — and why it has produced such a high level of good will. These factors help account not only for mentoring's meteoric rise, but for the euphoric expectations that have attended it.

Answering the Call

Cynthia Forest works for a law firm in Philadelphia. An African-American woman in her middle thirties, she is mentor to Keisha, a seventeen-year-old, through the Philadelphia Futures program.

She's a very nice girl, very polite, very bright, articulate. I feel very attached. But sometimes I feel like she's blowing smoke in my face. She doesn't want to disappoint me, so she says things that she knows I want to hear, yet she doesn't follow through. She dropped out of school just before the tenth grade this year and went to live with her boyfriend and his family. I finally got her to go back in January, but she dropped out again. So they suggested I take another student who's in school. But you can't desert her now, she needs mentoring more than ever.

I've told her in no uncertain terms: I'm here, I'll do whatever I can, bend over three times for you, but you've just got to work with me. I've gone pretty far—I said, "If you just get through high school I will personally see to it that you go to the college of your choice"—I mean, I don't know how I'm going to do it, but I'll cross that bridge when I get to it. But that's just how important it is to me, to just get her through high school.

Except for me and one other person, all of the mentors are white and all the kids are black inner-city youth. I think the race difference is an obstacle, but I really think that it's all about really wanting to make a difference. If you really want to bad enough and if you're in it for the right reasons, I think you can make it work regardless of the obstacles. That's my deep belief.

But all of us have had some tough times. Breaking the ice initially, you're taking two strangers, with the mentor saying, "I'm here for you" and all, and the kid who's probably looking at them like, "What planet is this person from?"

And the kids don't respond back, don't call back. You want the kid to call back and look as if they're interested, and the kid doesn't—95 percent of the time the kid doesn't call you. And I'm curious to find out why it is that they don't. Is it that they're really somewhat intimidated? Is it they're thinking, "The mentors want it more than I do, so let them come out to me?" I think maybe until a really good rapport is established, you're just not going to have the kid calling. Even now, my young person will call me on occasion, but not real often.

Across the board, we're putting in a lot more than the young persons are, but, you know, I think that should be expected, we're more responsible in a sense. That's a given. You're expected to give a lot more. And I'll tell you, you're going to have to be the type of person that's not going to be discouraged. You want to throw in the towel so often, especially when you feel like you're not getting through. A lot of times you feel like you're in this thing by yourself.

The kids are so used to people not sticking around that they figure, "Well, this is just another one." But if you really, really care and meet the rejection, in the end this person realizes that you didn't just walk away, you're there, you really still care. And then it's a very, very gradual thing, they begin to trust you, to trust that you're going to be there for them. So it's just stick to it, keep going no matter what.

She did something really special on Valentine's Day—she came by the job, dropped by, sort of unannounced, with a Valentine's card and a little gift—it was a ring and a little key chain that said "I Love You." I almost burst into tears, I was so touched.

With all the obstacles, I think we have a really good relationship—she knows I'm there, and I know that she's there too.

5

The Benefits
of Mentoring

*People who grew up in difficult circumstances and yet
are successful have one thing in common: at a critical
juncture in their early adolescence, they had a positive
relationship with a caring adult.*
  —Bill Clinton,
  president of the United States

*M*entoring's ability to mobilize a diverse group of supporters
and to inspire dramatic claims for its transforming powers brings
into focus an essential question: what are a group of middle-
class volunteers likely to accomplish through forming one-to-
one relationships with young people living in poverty? Before
looking closely at the experience of mentors in mentoring programs, it is useful to examine what social science can tell us about
the value of natural mentors in helping poor kids.

One Good Relationship

Over the past decade a converging body of research across a
variety of disciplines strongly suggests that relationships matter, that bonds with caring adults can make an important difference in the lives of vulnerable youth as they navigate their way

toward adulthood. The richest evidence comes from psychologists studying "resilient" youth, young people who manage to weather the storms of poverty and go on to make it as self-sufficient adults. These young people, the Sean Varners of the world, are able to endure intensive pressures, rebound from collapse, and continue pushing forward.

Researchers focusing on how these youths are buffered from surrounding stress and turmoil point to a triad of protective factors that recurs in their stories. The first is the personality and social responsiveness of the youth; the second is the presence of close-knit, cohesive, and supportive families. The third element consists of extra-familial sources of support, such as community mentors. Resilient youth appear skilled at recruiting and developing these sources, particularly when the family leg of the triad is weakened or removed entirely. Like Sean, these youths are skilled at reaching out to people like Miss Taylor the guidance counselor or mentors like John Hogan as these opportunities for support present themselves.[1]

Norman Garmezy and researchers at the University of Minnesota report the critical importance of at least one significant adult, usually an extra-familial adult, in the development of inner-city youth.[2] In one examination of children of war, Garmezy and his colleagues find nonfamilial adults to be of prime importance in helping youth handle stress, noting that "such adults provide for the children a representation of their efficacy and the demonstrable ability to exert control in the midst of upheaval."[3]

In a series of epidemiological studies in Great Britain, psychiatrist Sir Michael Rutter of the University of London maintains that children in dysfunctional settings who have one good relationship are at lower risk of psychiatric disorder. In another study, of low-income black children from divorced or separated families, Rutter finds the influence of grandparents to be linked to lower dropout rates, leading him to speculate that the strength and quality of the relationship may be more important than whether the adult is a parent or even a relative, that "good relationships outside the family can have a protective effect similar to that which apparently stems from within the immediate family."[4]

The most substantial research pointing to the protective role of unrelated adults is the work of Emmy E. Werner of the University of California, Davis. Werner's thirty-year longitudinal study of five hundred children growing up on a sugar plantation on the Hawaiian island of Kauai shows that without exception, the young people who survived this environment, characterized by persistent poverty and high incidences both of alcoholism and mental illness among parents, were able to draw on the support of neighborhood mentors, frequently unrelated adults. Werner argues that with "the help of these support networks, the resilient children developed a sense of meaning in their lives and a belief that they could control their fate."[5] Werner concludes that "research on resilient children has shown repeatedly that if a parent is incapacitated or unavailable, other significant people in a young child's life can play an enabling role." She goes on to argue that in such situations, "it may make better sense to strengthen such available informal ties to kin and community," than to add new layers of bureaucracy or social services.

Developmentalists further argue that adolescence may be a critical time for the introduction of unrelated adult models and mentors, as young people are redefining their relationship to parents and undergoing fundamental physiological, psychological, and sexual changes. Carol Gilligan of Harvard contends that "relationships between girls and adult women may be particularly critical during the transition into adolescence," stating that youth at this juncture are eager to "seek out and listen attentively to advice from women."[6] Rutter adds that while parent-child relationships in early childhood are extremely valuable for healthy development, adolescence offers a chance to catch up, a turning point where successful relationships with others "may change the life course onto a more adaptive trajectory."[7]

Alongside these scholars, psychologists looking at other aspects of youth development also emphasize the importance of mentoring relationships. Mary Ainsworth, a principal figure in the subdiscipline focusing on children's attachment to others, asserts that unrelated adults can play an important role in the lives of youth, particularly "in the case of children who find in such relationships the security they could not attain with their own parent."[8] Stanford University researcher Albert Bandura, who studies identification, argues that during later stages of development mentors are critical for young people in their attempt to prepare for new social roles, such as those in the workplace.[9] Social support researchers have long emphasized the importance of informal, nonprofessional caregivers, or extra-familial helping figures, as sources of help to the poor, particularly in times of crisis.[10]

Echoing Elijah Anderson's description of the importance of "old heads," urban anthropologists similarly stress the functions of mentors in the socialization and development of inner-city youth. In *Growing Up Poor,* for example, Terry Williams and William Kornblum follow the life histories of nine hundred teenagers in New York, Cleveland, Louisville, and Meridian, Mississippi, looking at the various pathways communities offered their young people out of poverty. They argue that most young people can either make it despite many disadvantages or remain mired in poverty. Williams and Kornblum conclude that the common denominator among those who make it is the presence of caring adults: "The probabilities that teenagers will end up on the corner or in a stable job are conditioned by a great many features of life in their communities. Of these, we believe the most significant is the presence or absence of adult mentors."[11]

Bernard Lefkowitz, interviewing some five hundred at-risk youth, writes in *Tough Change:* "Again and again, I found that the same pattern was repeated: The kid who managed to climb out of the morass of poverty and social pathology was the kid who found somebody, *usually in school,* sometimes outside, who helped them invent a promising future. In practical terms, the presence of the understanding, concerned, yet demanding mentor transforms the meaning and quality of education."[12]

The accumulation of these findings, along with various social, cultural, and political influences discussed in earlier chapters, have led many to conclude that we must provide more mentors for young people in poverty. President Clinton states that if these mentors are not present in the young person's immediate environment, then society has the responsibility to provide access to such individuals.

The mentoring movement is an attempt to do so, intentionally, through the use of volunteers — to engineer adult-youth relationships while attempting to preserve the benefits observed in so many natural settings. Proponents argue not only that this objective is possible but that it is practical at great scale and at low cost.

But questions remain. Professor Jean Rhodes of the University of Illinois observes that while "natural mentor relationships typically emerge from within the youth's social support network," assigned relationships are grafted onto this existing network. She adds that it is also unclear whether resilient youth do well because they find mentoring relationships — or whether these youth find mentoring relationships, and use them well, because they possess some third quality. It may take more than simply making adult relationships available to dramatically increase the resilience of additional youths.[13]

Definitive answers to these and other mysteries of mentoring have yet to be found. However, from a variety of sources — including program evaluations, interviews with participants, and observation of mentoring in action — it is possible to begin piecing together a rough understanding about what formal, matched, cross-class, one-to-one mentoring can and cannot do to help.

The remainder of this chapter takes a closer look at the benefits young people appear to derive from participation in one-to-one programs. It confirms that mentoring efforts address very real needs among youth for adult caring and personal attention. It further suggests that it is possible for middle-class volunteers both to forge significant one-to-one relationships with low-income youth and to provide them valuable assistance in the process.

Forging Connections

As stated, the experience of mentoring programs encourages the possibility of establishing bonds between adults and youth through the one-to-one process. Programs reveal not only a substantial percentage of relationship formation — there is evidence to suggest that between one-third and two-thirds of matches lead to relationships — but that the bonds formed range considerably in nature and intensity.

Without attempting a precise cataloguing of these relationships, it is possible to see them on a continuum. On one end resides what might be called primary relationships, in the middle are secondary relationships, and at the other end of the spectrum are those pairings that never take hold.

Primary relationships are characterized by extraordinary commitment, intensity, and emotional openness. These partners become, essentially, fictive kin, and their relationship looks a lot like the classical conception of mentoring described earlier. In the case of primary relationships, while the mentoring program functions as the route to connection, these bonds quickly move well beyond the walls of the program.

One seventeen-year-old high school student in the Cleveland Career Beginnings program has established a primary relationship. She describes her mentor as being "like a parent away from home . . . someone you can lean on for awhile and who can lean on you." Another teenager, in a mentoring program for young mothers in Portland, Maine, chooses a combination of terms to characterize her primary mentor: "She's like my best friend, my mom, the whole works." As Sean Varner describes it — even if the mentoring program ceased to exist, were "to blow up," his relationship with John would continue — these connections are both intense and enduring. They recall Howell Raines's characterization of mentoring as "a kinship of choice."

More common in mentoring programs are secondary bonds. They differ from primary relationships, first, in being much less primary. Neither mentor nor youth are a major focus of each other's life, residing rather on the periphery along with other secondary interests, activities, and acquaintanceships. Mentors and youth in secondary relationships are friendly, but neither intimate nor committed to a longer-term bond. If the program were "to blow up," it is unlikely that these partners would continue meeting for very long. The position of mentors in secondary relationships tends to be specific and tangible, that of a helpful good neighbor, concerned about the circumstances of the youths, willing to take some time to assist them, but careful about maintaining clear boundaries.

One mentor in Michigan illustrates these borders, stating that "[The student] wants to pursue the relationship, but I don't think it is a good idea for her or for any of the other students and me and the other mentors to mix up our private lives with our positions here." She focuses on improving her grades through tutoring and other highly specified tasks. Youths in secondary relationships, similarly, maintain functional goals and clear emotional limits. They look to the mentors for help in finding jobs, doing homework, and applying to college, but do not cultivate deep emotional involvement.

Distinguished from primary and secondary bonds are matches where no relationship forms. These adults and youths never connect, oftentimes never even meet, as the match disintegrates either in frustration or lack of interest.

Making a Difference

Just as the experience of mentoring programs suggests the possibility of making a connection, it affirms as well, that mentors can make a difference. One source of evidence is the small body of program evaluation in existence. A national study of the Career Beginnings demonstration — which includes a number of components in addition to mentoring — shows students with mentors attending college on schedule at a higher rate than a control group.[14] An evaluation of Project RAISE, conducted by researchers at Johns Hopkins, finds RAISE students improving attendance and grades in English in comparison to controls.[15] A third study, of the Atlanta Adopt-a-Student program, reveals young people with mentors as more likely to enroll in postsecondary education. An array of other studies, many of them based on self-reported information, also suggest a link between mentoring and improvements in the lives of young people.[16]

When one looks more closely both at research and the day-to-day experience of mentors and youth, it is possible to discern a range of positive developments linked to mentoring, with important benefits congregating in three particular areas.

Supplying Information and Opportunities

At the most basic level, mentors broaden the horizons of youth, exposing them to new experiences beyond what is currently available in their lives. In this respect they act as a bridge to the out-side world, a world not often accessible or even visible to young people growing up in the inner city. This process can amount to a tour of middle-class life.

One of the first stops on this tour is the world of work. Ben Warren remembers growing up knowing what the corner store was like, but with little sense of the corporate world. He is intent on making sure his mentee, Jamal, gets to see this world from the inside. John Hogan makes sure Sean gets to meet his friends who are working in a wide array of fields, in order to make a variety of career options more tangible.

College education is also an area where many mentors are active in their assistance to youth. Mentors help youths navigate the maze of applications, test taking, financial aid, and selection, assistance that is oftentimes not available from any other source. Some go even further. Sandy Lawrence, for ex-ample, gets her company's travel agent to find a complimentary ticket for Teri so that the student can interview at the Univer-sity of Arizona. Later, she helps Teri hook up with a summer preparation program at Kenyon College designed to help ease the transition to the freshman year.

In addition to vocational and educational assistance, men-tors also provide other forms of cultural and social exposure. Eileen Benton, a mentor in Baltimore, involves her student, Jer-ome, in her family life: "Mostly we go to my home — my daugh-ter and husband are involved — and we do things together. My husband plays basketball with him, or they wash the car . . . we've gone to the zoo . . . he goes grocery shopping with me, helps set the table, just things he's not used to." Beyond expos-ing youth to options, many mentors actively try to help them take advantage of opportunities through developing their sense of competence. They tutor the youngsters, coach them on job interviews, help them strategize and develop their problem solv-ing skills.

Many mentors also become involved in advocacy on be-half of their students, making sure they get the kind of treat-ment in schools, for example, that middle-class kids have come to expect. One mentor illustrates: "Ronald got suspended. Three or four kids were throwing ketchup in the lunch room. Not a life-threatening event, but he got suspended. His mother did not know the rules. Like most people, she thought that if you're suspended, you're automatically out of school for three days. In reality, a mother can just call the principal; if the event is not serious, the student is reinstated immediately. I found out about the suspension the second day, and got Ronald's mother to call. He was let back into school right away, and only missed a day."

In situations such as these, mentors' familiarity with how to navigate bureaucracies, coupled with the alienation and intimidation many low-income parents feel toward schools, fills an important gap for students. Not only does Ronald get someone who is in his corner, but a crisis is averted. Suspension would have resulted in missing several days of school, returning to class behind, and increasing the chances of disengagement on Ronald's part — repeating a pattern in school the mentor was already working hard to counteract.

Providing Nurturance and Support

After working one-on-one with a high school student for over a year, Michal Young, a mentor in Washington, D.C. states: "These kids, they really do need somebody to talk to. Not so much somebody to hug and hold them necessarily. But somebody to bounce their thoughts off of, and to know they're not the only ones feeling desperate and sorry and pitiful today, that this boyfriend that broke their heart is not the absolute end to their lives." She adds, "They can't get that kind of feedback from other fifteen-year-olds."

Her words echo the importance young people place on someone who is willing to sit down and listen to them. In focus group interviews, young people living in the inner city again and again register their desire "to talk to caring adults who can offer them advice and help them with problems."[17] In addition to providing a sympathetic ear, mentors supply affiliation and security for youth. They can also help them have fun, an aspect which can't be overestimated, given the deplorable quality of life so many face.

Sometimes a mentor's support can be conveyed in simple and unspoken ways. Sandy Lawrence goes to Teri's volleyball games; as she explains, "I'm one of the few adults there who is not a teacher and not a parent, and there are very few parents. All the kids know why I'm there, and I think that has an impact just from the standpoint of, 'Here's another adult who doesn't have to be here — who is here!'"

This support not only helps youth in the course of day-to-day life, but can be especially important at times of crisis, which can lead to a downward spiral for young people without much support. In fact, such times can serve to cement the mentoring relationship, as one young person, recalling the death of her boyfriend, explains: "The day that it happened she [her mentor] was right over and she gave me a great big hug and asked me if I was all right, and if I was going to be all right, which really helped me out. I really didn't think we were that close until that happened and she was right there."

Over time, successful mentors move from simple support to a complex version involving what Makarenko, a Russian educator, calls "the maximum of support with the maximum of challenge." Uri Bronfenbrenner argues that this combination is "essential . . . if children are to avoid alienation and develop into capable young adults."[18] It is reflected in many mentors' comments, as they talk about providing "tough love" or a "gentle firmness" for youth, about combinations of nurturing love and high expectations, unconditional support and consistent accountability.

Preparing Youth for Adulthood

Mentors help young people grow up. On the most practical level this means helping them think through important decisions like what careers they will pursue. For example, Eileen Benton tries to get her student, Jerome, to think about life after school: "His career goals are to be either a rapper or a basketball player. I say, 'You know you're short. I don't think there's much hope for a basketball career, and I'm really not sure there's really a career in rapping, so let's think of something else that we can work toward, just in case these two don't turn out.'"

Many mentors delve even more deeply into the requirements of growing up. Ben Warren explains that he and Jamal started out talking about surface issues such as sports. As they got closer, their conversations turned increasingly to personal issues, particularly concerning the opposite sex: "Into speaking about girls, what to do about girls . . . at some points, we talk about really decent things; other times, we talk about guy stuff—that's what a mentor's for."

In these and other ways, mentors are active socializers of youth, often serving as mediators, filtering various messages they receive and helping them make sense of their world in a way that builds self-esteem and social competence. As Erwin Flaxman explains: "Many minority youth . . . must make conflicting choices between the values, accepted behaviors, and attitudes of their own group and those of the larger society. These youth must choose between assimilation, separation, and alienation from the larger society or a kind of biculturalism. . . . Not having the maturity or a fully integrated identity, they need guidance and support to evaluate these choices." Mentors can be instrumental in developing the kind of bicultural competence many young people will require to navigate the very different worlds of their neighborhood and that of mainstream society.

Helping Youth Cope

In these various ways, mentors assume many of the functions Anderson associates with the "old head." They supplement the influences of parents and others, and begin to replenish some of the nutrients which were once more available in the natural life of many inner-city communities.

Mentors who form primary relationships are in a position not only to provide circumscribed forms of help—specific information, tangible resources, episodes of advocacy—but to effect more fundamental development. As Ronald Ferguson argues, "When youths know that adults really care and are not simply 'in it for the money' (a recurring phrase) they usually lower their defenses, pay attention, and accept help." These adults connect with young people at an emotional level, allowing them to achieve what Amos Smith, a social worker in Hartford, calls "the master key."[19]

Mentors who achieve the master key, as well as mentors in more secondary relationships, can all contribute in varying degrees to the ability of inner-city youth to cope with very difficult circumstances. They manage to do so by helping shift the balance between protective and risk factors present in the young person's life, serving, in James Garbarino's words, "to keep the challenge facing these chldren within the limits of their ability to cope."[20] Indeed, this is one of the basic reasons we intervene in the lives of young people, to prevent the build-up of risk factors that can make it impossible for even the most resilient of youth to keep landing on their feet.[21]

Answering the Call

Michal Young, married to John Hogan, is an African-American woman in her thirties. A physician affiliated with Georgetown University, she mentors a fifteen-year-old student, Robin, through the Mentors, Inc. program.

There's a saying that unto whom much is given, much is expected.

Well, Shayne [Schneider, the program director] and I used to talk a little bit about what was wrong with the world and things that were going on, and we always used to say that if somebody could just hold these kids' hands sometimes, not dragging them along, but just walking along with them, that maybe a lot of them wouldn't fall out of the way. So when she called me, she said, "Okay, Michal, now's the time for you to put your action where your mouth is." It was like a call to my convictions: "Do you really believe what you're saying?"

When I signed up, I really didn't anticipate the emotional investment of mentoring, the amount of it. You can't help but emotionally invest in the young person. It's not so much the time, although it is a lot of time, it's the emotional part.

I sometimes envy John and Sean [Michal's husband, John Hogan, and Sean Varner]. Robin and I have struggled. The first issue was trust; I want to say trust, but trust isn't quite the word for it. I had to do all the calling initially, for at least six months, eight months. It wasn't until the Mentors, Inc. picnic that she called me and asked me was I going and could she get a ride with me. That was the first time, almost eight months into the program. And it can be a little defeating to wait that long.

It's hard to get her to talk. You can say, "How's school going?" "It's okay." "Any boyfriend trouble?" "Ahh, no." I'm not a real conversationalist like my husband, John. John can talk about anything. And I don't have that gift. So it's been two personalities that tend not to talk, with Robin and me, and I have had to be the one reaching, and it took a little while—a long while. We still don't interact the way I envisioned, but you walk into it with your ideas about how it should work, and then it falls into where it's really going to be.

I've never really considered giving up, but I did step back and say, "Well, maybe she doesn't really want as much interaction as I want or I think she's going to need," so I had to just ease back and let her set the pace. And she has, to some extent. She'll call here and there. I called Friday and left a message and she didn't call me back, I haven't heard from her this weekend, this week. I had her babysit for me a couple of weeks ago, and she was happy to do that and we talked. But it's sporadic.

She gave me a Christmas present last year and this year, and I was surprised, I wasn't expecting to get anything of that kind. And when she decided that she was not going back to school, her mother came into the picture. Her mother called me because Robin had decided she wasn't going back to school in January, she was going to stay out a year, she needed a rest. And it took all of us to try to keep encouraging her. I said some pretty tough things to her, but she continued to stick with it. If she was going to slam the door that would have been the time.

She likes children and wants to be a pediatrician, that's why they put her with me. But I really don't think she has much of a chance. Her grades are not good and I am trying to get her to look at all the things that you can do to work with children, in addition to being a pediatrician. I said when I went to school to be a pediatrician I took a major in teaching because the reality was that I may have had to come out and teach and do a couple of other things before I could go on to medical school. So you have to prepare so that you could do a couple of things in case you don't get to your goal right away.

If I've made a difference in her life, it's been around babies

74

and boyfriends; we got into a pretty intense conversation about that one because she had decided she wasn't going to have any children until she was nineteen and I had to catch myself, because I realized for her and her colleagues—everybody on her street except her is pregnant or has been pregnant, some are working on their second child—nineteen was a long time. I said, "Nineteen, that sounds good, but I don't hear you saying anything to me about being married, you know, having a husband to father this baby."

She told me I'm old-fashioned like her mother, that's what she told me. And that was funny to me because me and my mother used to quarrel a bit and I never would have thought that I'd be considered old-fashioned.

I guess I knew many young people had perspectives like this, but I didn't know them this close. And you can see the hazard that it puts them in. I know that's one of the things that I have gotten from this mentoring relationship. Nothing in my training as a pediatrician really prepared me to fully understand, but this relationship has hit home. The things that I have tried to help Robin with have to do with lifestyle and the way you look at things, and trying to change those kinds of things at fifteen is a tough row to hoe. It's possible, but it's not likely.

6

The Limits
of Mentoring

If mentoring is pursued as a solution to "at-risk"
youth, it will fail to meet that mission, funding will
dry up, people will lose their enthusiasm and programs
will wither and be replaced by the next buzzword
solution.

— Shayne Schneider,
founder, Mentors, Inc.

*A*s heartening as it is to affirm that volunteer mentoring programs can result in relationships that make a difference for some
youth — that mentoring can contribute to helping young people
cope — the experience of these programs nevertheless provides
eloquent testimony to the difficulty of doing either. Quite simply, *mentoring is hard work,* a reality rarely conveyed amid all the
fervor surrounding this movement.

It is a reality, however, about which mentors speak une-
quivocally. Cynthia Forest observes that those who expect to waltz
in and transform lives will be in for a shock, adding that this
enterprise is often an endurance test: "You have to be the type
of person that's not going to be discouraged. You want to throw
in the towel so often, especially when you feel like you're not
getting through."

The Difficulty of Connecting

In the first place, the struggle is often simply to forge a connection. After calling a random selection of mentors a year into the program, A. C. Hubbard, board chair of Project RAISE in Baltimore, was shocked at how few were still involved: "I found a lot of frustration or inability to get through to kids, or that their time was such that they couldn't meet what we thought was a minimum. . . . A lot of them felt guilty." An independent evaluation of RAISE conducted by McPartland and Nettles of Johns Hopkins confirms Hubbard's impressions: "Recruiting mentors and having them sustain successful relationships with at-risk students has been a major challenge for most RAISE sponsors."[1]

Al Abromovitz, director of Cleveland's Career Beginnings program, says that he now shoots for a 50 percent connection rate, but admits that "if we have 180 matches and 70 are working, I'm happy." He used to lament these numbers until somebody pointed out that they compare favorably with the divorce rate. An informal survey of other program operators suggests that the proportion of matches that turn into significant relationships hovers between one-third to two-thirds overall — with the lower end more prevalent at programs engaging young people who are severely disadvantaged. One program operator described a high incidence of "phantom mentors."

Researchers echo these observations. Stephen Hamilton and Mary Agnes Hamilton of Cornell University began their study of the mentoring program Linking Up "to understand and trace the formation of mentoring relationships." However, after surveying the program's actual experience, they shifted their focus: "We sought instead to understand why so many pairs did not seem to be working out."[2]

Ronald Ferguson, too, found volunteer mentoring to be a struggle in most community programs. While "most programs hoped to use volunteer mentors to supplement the love and attention that their paid staffs provide to children," they were plagued by recruitment and attrition problems. Ferguson adds,

"Those that have tried have experienced only limited success at finding mentors and keeping them active."[3] A study of the Campus Partners in Learning mentoring program by Joseph Tierney and Alvia Branch of Public/Private Ventures reports that only 35 percent of the pairs met regularly, while 43 percent met only once or twice or not at all.[4]

Two problems that make it difficult for mentors and youth to connect are limited time and social distance. First, mentoring is bound up in a paradox concerning time. Much of mentoring's currency emanates from the growing concern that adults in our society are too busy to spend time with kids. However, in the words of Hamilton and Hamilton, efforts to "fill the gap run directly into the problems that created it."[5] The adults who volunteer as mentors don't have time to spend with the young people with whom they are matched.

This problem is particularly acute because the adults targeted by mentoring programs are often the same individuals whose work soaks up all their time. These are lawyers, managers, physicians, and other professional "role models" who are putting in sixty, seventy, or even eighty hours a week on the job and often do not have time to spend with their own kids.

In *The Overworked American,* Harvard economist Juliet Schor demonstrates that Americans work harder than any other country in the world, with the exception of Japan. Not only are two-income households the norm, but each individual worker is toiling longer hours. Since 1970, for example, the average American worker now puts in an estimated 164 more hours of paid labor annually—equivalent to an additional month of work. The result, according to Schor, is "a profound structural crisis of time" for Americans.[6] This structural crisis not only makes it more difficult to relax, but makes it more difficult to undertake what economist Robert Kuttner calls "the diverse unpaid activities that a viable society necessarily requires, from civic participation to voluntary caring for the young and the old."[7]

Given the competing commitments and countervailing forces pulling at these mentors, it is not surprising that Big Brothers/Big Sisters nationally has forty thousand young people on the waiting list—while seventy thousand are matched.

It is also no surprise that even the most committed and exceptional mentors find it challenging to sustain their involvement. In general, mentors are much better at signing up than showing up.

However, the failure to connect comes not just from mentors, but from students as well. Forging a relationship takes two people, and programs have experienced just as much difficulty getting young people to show up and stick with it.

First, many youths, even those in great need of support, are wary of adults — having been let down by them in the past, and living in environments where violence and other forms of abuse are common. Furthermore, mentoring is often an unfamiliar notion to these youth. As a result, many young people are slow to embrace these relationships, and the initiative often rests with the mentors.

However, it is often difficult to contact youth living in poverty. Many do not have a telephone, much less an answering machine. And teenagers are notoriously bad about returning phone calls, even when they get the message and have access to a phone.

The difficulty in getting middle-class mentors and disadvantaged youth to spend sufficient time together is all the more problematic because of the great gulfs that exist between their worlds. Mentors and youth must bridge this divide before they can forge a connection. As one adult observes, "We mentors represent such a foreign life to them. . . . I know she hears what I say, she remembers things, and she attempts to ask questions . . . but the connection is limited."

This comment cuts to the issue of social distance, present in varying degrees in most orchestrated mentoring relationships that bring together mainstream adults and poor youth. This distance begins with a generation gap. It is often accentuated by life-style differences, and in many cases, by ethnic background as well. But the most profound distance, which is shared by mentors of varying ages and ethnic backgrounds, is that of class.

The successful "role models" targeted as mentors often have little in common with the youth. Unfamiliar worlds collide; different languages are spoken. The partners react in ways that are perplexing to each other. Often neither has known anyone like the other before. Not surprisingly, the potential for misunderstanding is considerable.

In reviewing the literature on mentoring, Ascher, Flaxman, and Harrington of Columbia University's Institute on Urban and Minority Education comment that in settings where social distance is great, the mentors' world can easily seem "irrelevant or even nonsensical" to the youngsters, "and their goals for the mentees naive."[8] This perspective is supported by a number of new studies appearing since 1990 detailing an oppositional culture among many inner-city youth that makes connection very difficult. These studies portray youth of "the hip-hop generation" as profoundly alienated from mainstream society, not only white society but middle-class black society as well.

A 1992 report funded by the Robert Wood Johnson Foundation and based on extensive focus groups with inner-city youth depicts a group of young people inured to the messages of leaders emphasizing safe sex or drug avoidance: "The African-American urban teenager may well be the most difficult audience to reach with an antiabuse or prosocial message. Mainstream society has virtually no credibility with these young people; they are alienated from their own heritage, and their subculture tolerates self-destructive behavior and encourages taking risks."[9]

Studying low-income urban black teenagers in Boston, psychologist Richard Majors of the University of Wisconsin describes what he terms "the cool pose" adopted by so many young black males in the inner city. Majors traces the origin of the cool pose to attempts on the part of youth to maintain a sense of pride and identity in a hostile society. However, he also shows how the pose can isolate young people from the kind of support critical for nurturance and development; Majors states, for example, that "some black males have difficulty disclosing their deepest feelings even to their best friends and girlfriends."[10]

Resilient, Receptive, Resistant:
John Hogan's Story, Continued

The experience of John Hogan, which in many ways epitomizes the mentoring ideal, actually contributes to cultivating a balanced picture of the range of experiences mentors encounter. John's relationship with Sean illustrates the success that can be achieved in mentoring young people who are highly resilient, who might be called "mentor-prone"— possessing an internal ability to recruit mentors and make use of the mentoring situation. Every program includes a few young people, Sandy Lawrence's protégé, Teri, being another example, who are "reaching out" for mentors, poised to capitalize on this assistance.

However, these young people are a small minority of the program population. More prevalent are young people like Robin, the teenager with whom John's wife, Michal Young, is paired. If Sean is highly resilient — reaching out for a mentor — Robin might be termed receptive — reachable, but definitely not reaching out. It took Robin eight months to return Michal's phone calls, and even now the returned calls are sporadic. While Sean pursued John from the beginning, for Michal it was, at first, "a closed door." Over time that door slowly opened, and a relationship formed, but the mentoring process has been demanding.

As John Hogan reflects, "A lot of times you've got students who can't reach out, who've forgotten how. They're living in home situations where they must be independent, where they are forced to rely on themselves and their own resources."

John's understanding of this subject comes not only from Michal's experience, but from his own effort to connect with Sean's younger brother. Fifteen years old when John first met him, Hogan called this youth the "phantom" brother; it was a year and a half before he ever saw him. Hogan recalls telling Sean, "I said, 'You serious, this boy lives with you!' I mean no matter what time it was, what day of the week, Sunday, he was never there."

John recounts that when he finally did meet the phantom brother, he found him to be "a nice young man." "I told him, 'I'm gonna mentor you too.' I told him, 'I'm here, I'm ready,' I said, 'Call me some time.'" No calls were forthcoming, until one day when the teenager needed a ride downtown:

> One day he needed a ride to court and I took him.
> I just talked to him. I was open about things, about

his drugs. He told me he was gonna give up on the drugs. I said, "Do you really think you can turn away from that life-style, the money, the women, the fast pace, just turn and walk?" He said yeah. I said, "Brother, I'm gonna tell you something, I don't know if I could, and you at fifteen say you can. I'm all behind you if you can."

And he lasted a couple of weeks, but he was right back out there again and I haven't seen him anymore. I don't know where he is now. No matter how hard a mentor might try, he was out of reach.

Sean's brother illustrates that some youth — in contrast to those reaching out to mentors, or even those seemingly within reach — are simply out of reach. If Sean can be characterized as "resilient," and Robin "receptive," then Sean's brother might be termed "resistant." Resistant youth will not be reached by volunteer mentors in all but the most heroic and exceptional cases, an assertion supported by experience, particularly those efforts targeting the most disadvantaged.

The Difficulty of Making a Difference

While some youth clearly benefit from mentoring, often in rather dramatic ways, the research record is mixed. While the last chapter reported some of the more heartening aspects of studies, these results need qualification. While participants in the Adopt-a-Student program, for example, are slightly more likely to go on to college, they are no more likely to graduate from high school or find employment than a comparison group of students without mentors.

Studies of Milwaukee's One-on-One program and Baltimore's Project RAISE offer very sober findings. In the former study, a local research firm concluded that "most students in the program did not show an improvement in grades during the program year, although this was one of the program's primary objectives."[11] In the latter case, researchers found that most RAISE students remained far below average for Baltimore County schools in academic performance and at risk of dropping out. No impacts were recorded on standardized test scores or promotion rates; indeed, 40 percent of the students flunked the ninth grade. These results led the researchers to conclude that while the program had helped with "impressive gains in school attendance and in report card marks," this progress is not nearly "sufficient to eliminate the academic risks with which students entered the program."[12]

Echoing these findings, participants and program operators suggest that it is often just as difficult to make a difference as it is to make a connection. RAISE program managers are reevaluating their goals in light of "too many deficits to be overcome . . . [and] too few resources."[13] Reflecting on the program's effects after four years, Buzzy Hettleman, director of the effort and former Maryland Commissioner of Human Resources, concludes that mentoring is simply not enough for many young people living in poverty; he adds that it is also very difficult to find mentors who will make a one-year commitment to meet young people who are at risk on a twice-a-month basis.

In explaining why it is so difficult to make a difference, participants and program staff point to the formidable realities of poverty, which exercise considerable influence on the prospects of young people growing up in low-income, inner-city neighborhoods. Although the testimony of mentors and others underscores the point that mentoring addresses real and profound needs, these needs are often so profound that mentoring can seem, in the words of one mentor, like a "drop in the bucket."

Richard Morris, a businessman and mentor in Milwaukee's One-on-One program, considers his own experience and that of fellow Rotary Club members who have come forward to volunteer: "None of us understood the kind of kids that we'd be working with and the challenges that would be brought forth. We had these expectations, you know. We're all pretty macho. We'd walk in there and we figured, at least I did, that if I just lend this young person a little bit of the wonderfulness that I have in my brain, that they're automatically going to respond and be terrific. And the reality is that it is absolutely not true."

Morris concludes that mentoring will not make a great

impact on a great number of students. He feels this way because "we're talking about survival of these kids, trying to bring them from . . . utter failure and utter chaos, to a place where they have some self-esteem and self-image and hopefulness."

Ben Warren, recalling how tough it was to grow up in North Philadelphia fifteen years ago, admits "you'd have to call that fun compared to today's standards." Mentor Sharon Steiner describes the challenges she's confronting in trying to help her student in 1990 Baltimore, comparing it with 1980 Houston, where she was a Big Sister to a girl living in public housing. The deterioration of conditions in public housing and the social and economic environment in which these children are growing up leaves her far less optimistic than she felt ten years earlier.

Many mentors despair that it is too late to intervene once the youths are in their teens. Gerald Green, a mentor in Washington, states that it has been both difficult and overwhelming to "take somebody on at this late stage and try to bring a focus into their lives. I started with Diego when he had just finished the tenth grade, and I have come to the conclusion that's just too late; you just can't turn things around at that point." Coming to similar conclusions, the operators of Project RAISE have started working with second- and third-graders in a new incarnation of the project, attempting to provide them mentors through the beginning of high school.

Most of these mentors are forced to accept that, given present circumstances, the prospects of dramatic change, of recreating the Sean Varner/John Hogan saga of success, are limited. In this spirit, Ascher, Flaxman, and Harrington warn that while youth may be isolated, they do not reside in a vacuum. These researchers caution that mentoring will not "pluck adolescents out of poor homes, inadequate schools, or disruptive communities. . . . Thus the power of other influences in the lives of youth must be recognized in any attempt to reasonably measure the potential accomplishments of mentoring." They conclude that this strategy is best seen as a "modest intervention."[14]

Susan Phillips, director of the Greater Milwaukee Education Trust, which oversees the One-on-One mentoring program, concurs: "If you've got a child who's been failed since kindergarten . . . your chances of turning that child around in less than a year are nearly impossible." Even mentors in strong relationships discover that they are only one influence among many; these young lives are not easily transformed.[15]

The Risks of Failure for Youth and Adults

A 1990 article in the *Wall Street Journal* begins, "As any pupil who has brought the teacher an apple can testify," the mentoring process can be "fitfully complex" and filled with potential frictions. The article continues, "When these relationships work, they're fabulous. But when they don't work, they can be terribly destructive."[16]

This is a rare observation; the pitfalls of mentoring are usually ignored. Sharan Merriam notes that in the corporate world, "only successful mentoring relationships have been reported."[17] Healy and Welchert report that their literature review of mentoring in the corporate and education arenas repeatedly confronted "a tautological definition of mentoring that produced positively biased samples." In other words, individuals interviewed for studies were questioned only about positive mentoring experience, a practice that means "we do not learn from the failures."[18]

Reluctance to address the downsides and risks of mentoring characterizes the current wave of youth mentoring as well. For the most part, mentoring is portrayed, in the words of a *USA Today* headline, as a "win-win proposition."[19] Yet, in reality, both sides in mentoring programs risk losses. When acknowledged, the risks are usually posed as related to abuse, particularly sexual abuse. Out of this concern, Boy Scouts of America will not allow an adult to be alone, one-to-one, with a young person. On the other side there is also concern for the safety of volunteers, especially when working with young people in low-income neighborhoods.

The most prevalent risks of mentoring, however, are less tangible. On one side, the young people in mentoring programs are accustomed to being let down by adults, but are being asked to trust yet again. When the youth do let their guard down, they are all too often disappointed by mentors who keep them at arm's length, who don't show up, who don't follow through. On the adult side, disappointment is also destructive, even if it is less willingly admitted or discussed. Armand Waters, a youth worker in the One-on-One program in Milwaukee, is blunt in asking, "What are mentors going to do when one of these kids — and I've had it happen to me — turns around and calls them a dirty M-F?"

Shayne Schneider, founder of Mentors, Inc. in Washington, D.C., answers, "Their feelings get hurt. They say that they don't, but I believe they do." Schneider tries to warn people in advance about the distinct possibility that youth will be resistant, indifferent, or even hostile: "I tell them all the reasons why teenagers don't return phone calls, but they still think it's that their kid doesn't like them." This is true for some of the most prominent mentors: "They come in like executives and they never let you know or never want to let you know how easily hurt they are. But many of the mentors who withdraw from the programs do so because their feelings have been hurt."

Almost all the programs contacted had stories of busy mentors who repeatedly took off from work to meet with their students, only to be stood up. And while Schneider admits that having your feelings hurt is "not a disaster like a nuclear war," she says that hurt can lead to anger and to the reinforcement of prejudices. Mentors often harbor dual feelings toward the youth, feelings of sympathy matched by those of antipathy. Unattended, hurt can fortify negative feelings while undermining the positive ones.

Missing Infrastructure

The barriers and risks of mentoring do not obviate its real usefulness as a strategy for aiding individual children. Identifying them, however, puts mentoring's broad-scale potential in perspective, correcting for the tendency to acknowledge only its more uplifting aspects.

In most instances, mentoring is, in fact, falling short of its potential. Built-in obstacles are compounded by a considerable lack of infrastructure in the field. Programs are struggling to implement publicized models, and actual practice is uneven. Most sorely missing is follow-up. While marketing and recruitment have proceeded apace, program support is often neglected. Mentors find themselves matched, then abandoned; oversight is commonly delegated to overburdened school counselors; all too often, the entire enterprise is held together by sheer force of will on the part of dedicated founders.

One of the great ironies of mentoring is that this strategy, so often sold as a corrective to the isolation of youth, is so often conducted in isolation. One mentor explains his surprise about "the degree to which I've been all alone in this." An observer of mentoring programs notes that "few programs have the resources to serve mentors as well as mentees."

While the absence of resources is perhaps most conspicuous, also commonly missing are operational experience, knowledge regarding effective practice, and an appreciation — more by those outside than inside programs — of how hard it is to put mentoring into action. The absence of program infrastructure, made much worse by pressures to grow quickly and produce miraculous results, compromises mentoring's real potential to help.

A Modest Intervention

While recent years have seen a significant increase in mentoring activity, and while some youth are clearly being helped in a variety of ways, a set of sobering cautions are in order. Mentoring is nowhere near the mass movement of millions that is often envisioned, and it is unlikely ever to be such a movement — the enterprise is simply too difficult and demanding. In addition, many relationships — perhaps half, perhaps even more — simply do not take hold. Furthermore, even in the cases where relationships between adults and youth do form, these bonds remain just one influence amid many on the lives of the youngsters. In practice, few lives are transformed. And finally, it is imperative to recognize the risks inherent in engineering relationships, particularly when trying to do so across a great social divide.

These assertions accord with an accumulation of research on voluntarism emerging from the 1980s. Surveying a decade of efforts, the Eisenhower Foundation, long a proponent of urban voluntarism, concludes: "Although we are sympathetic to the sentiment behind that approach, our experience — and it is by now extensive — tells us that while volunteers may be very *helpful* in the context of a well-designed and resourced program, voluntarism is crucially limited as a response to inner-city problems — particularly given the nature of the communities that are hardest hit by crime, youthful alienation, and drug abuse."[20]

This indictment is by no means restricted to voluntarism, but really extends to the entire universe of short-term efforts on behalf of children living in poverty. Over and over again the research findings are unmistakable: short-term interventions don't produce long-term impacts.[21]

As James Garbarino explains, there are no quick fixes for the poverty, deprivation, and despair confronting these young people. "Much as we would like to make the world new for them through some magical program," states Garbarino, this aspiration is simply out of reach: "We will console ourselves with helping them survive emotionally."[22]

Answering the Call

Sharon Steiner is an architect in Baltimore. A white woman in her late thirties, she mentors Rita, a black seventh-grader, through Project RAISE.

We mentors represent such a foreign life to the youth. I ask myself, "Would it matter if I were black, if I were in a blue-collar job?" Maybe that would make some difference, make me more immediate. I know she hears what I say, remembers things, and she attempts to ask questions or respond to things. But the connection is limited and by definition probably always will be.

One day Rita was at my house and we were sitting by the back window and she said, "Do you ever hear shots?" And I said, "What?" She said, "Shots, guns." And I said, "No." And she said, "My mother won't let us sit by the window in our house because of the guns." At that time they were living on the seventh floor of a high-rise building—but the guns were there, I'm sure of it.

She loves being around my place. When she first came over to my house, which by the standards of other RAISE mentors is very modest, she was amazed. She said, "Do you live here by yourself?" and I said, "Yes." And she had to think about it. At the time she was living in public housing, a three-bedroom apartment with eight people on top of each other and a noise level up to here. And I said, "I don't have a family to support, I just have to take care of myself and I don't have to buy school clothes and books and food for as many people as your mother does." Sometimes I think that, maybe, by seeing a woman living on her own, she may think, maybe if I don't have a child right away I'll be able to have a place by myself someday.

There are many weeks when I just think, "Oh, I don't want to do anything for anybody on the weekend," you know, but she says,

"Can we do something?" and I'll say, "Okay." And I don't spend huge amounts of time with the girl, but, it sounds corny but, invariably, when we're getting together, and afterwards, I really enjoy it. A lot of things we do are not so heavy academically as some other mentors. We do some homework and reports when she has them, but we also do other stuff. We bake together, I've taught her how to bake from scratch—which teaches her mathematics indirectly, and reading recipes and following directions. And she helps me in the garden, and there is a satisfaction in helping me plant and then see things come out of the ground.

I have to be very honest, and I would never say this in front of Rita, but I'm very worried, based on what I see today, as opposed to the situation of five or ten years ago as a Big Sister. I'm much more pessimistic. I've seen public housing now for many years, and the situation is much worse. And I've seen the social environment in which poor children are growing up over the years and it's much worse. I am appalled by the state of education in the country. I am appalled by the family setting in which many of these children are being raised.

And when I look at the situation Rita and the other kids in the program are facing, no amount of help from a mentor is going to overcome that environment. I do not believe in miracle cures. Mentoring is the proverbial drop in the bucket. I think it's helpful, I think it may help Rita stop and think occasionally and maybe, maybe out of this program some girls will take that extra effort to stay in school. There's a little more incentive.

Many of the mentors in this program are from privileged backgrounds. They have been isolated from the public schools, they sent their kids to private schools, and these people are shocked and amazed by what they encounter. I think a lot of them go into the program thinking we're going to turn these kids into middle-class kids, save them, and now they know that ain't going to happen, for a lot of different reasons. I probably had some of those illusions myself. And I realize that's just pie in the sky.

90

Another mentor in the program is very wealthy, drives a fancy car, and after the first meeting she refused to go to her student's place. She refuses to go to the public housing projects. She made her student get on the bus and come to her. You know, it's scary, but if you can't deal with these children's lives, then you better think about your involvement with them, because that is their reality! And you know, if we're going to let a thirteen-year-old girl in this society live in that environment, then we better be prepared to deal with those consequences.

Why do I keep going? One reason is my background. I'm a product of the late sixties and early seventies. I grew up politically motivated in Nashville, around the Southern Christian Leadership Conference and Martin Luther King and Bobby Kennedy. These were the heroes of my childhood and they mean something in my life. There's a piece of me that will never stop attempting to help because of what's in my background.

But at this point the strongest reason is a personal dedication to that little girl, to Rita. In whatever strange way we are friends, we are connected, now for a year and a half, and to suddenly step out of her life would be inexplicable and not very nice. I care about her.

7

Making the Most of Mentoring

*The house of delusions is cheap to build
but drafty to live in.*
—A. E. Housman,
London, 1892

The mismatch between mentoring's rhetoric and its modest results is not surprising, given the developmental stage of the field. The movement is in its infancy, and such start-up periods, as the experience of Big Brothers/Big Sisters and Friendly Visiting well attest, are renowned for overheated marketing. The primary objective is getting people's attention, and mentoring has undoubtedly succeeded on this score.

The disparity between rhetoric and reality is further to be expected, given the history of the mentoring concept in our culture. Mentoring inspires hyperbole, as the euphoria that attended the corporate wave confirms.

Fervor Without Infrastructure

As predictable as the gulf between rhetoric and reality might be, and as justifiable over the short term, the overselling of mentoring is a liability. It contributes to an approach that one observer calls "fervor without infrastructure," a view that amounts to the belief in simple solutions to complex problems and believes that the problems, no matter how exceptional, will go away in response to enough inspirational stories.

Fervor without infrastructure is dangerous at the program level because it leads to disappointed mentors and youth. It is dangerous at the policy level because it plays into the unfortunate tendency to lunge at new and glossy strategies, glorify them over the short term, and discard them as they tarnish. More disturbing is the way fervor without infrastructure feeds the recurring appetite for voluntarist panaceas, idealized in isolation from institutions, proposed as quick, cheap, and easy. As such, mentoring serves to distract attention from deep-seated problems that cannot be simply marketed away.

Fervor without infrastructure is a setup for failure and will inevitably lead mentoring to become just another good idea that did not work out. This pattern recalls the demise of Friendly Visiting, which rapidly ran the cycle from initial enthusiasm to bewildered disappointment. It is worth remembering that Friendly Visiting was undermined by enormous expectations in combination with a dearth of volunteers, difficulties in forging relationships across great social distance, and worsening economic circumstances.

The big losers in this cycle of disappointment will, of course, be impoverished young people, robbed again of yet another potential source of support. Indeed, in locations across the country, there are indications that just such a cycle may be playing out.

In Cleveland, Career Beginnings has been dropped by several corporations whose unrealistic expectations have not been fulfilled. Program director Al Abromovitz says that in these instances, "If we had ten mentors, there'd be a couple of magics and two or three others who were connecting." The rest were running into frustration. As a result, the corporations just pulled out. Abromowitz reflects, "If we don't meet the dream, they'll go on to something else."

In Milwaukee, after an early evaluation of the One-on-One program found the effort performing weakly against dramatic

goals, the *Milwaukee Journal* ran the headline, "New Project Gets
So-So Grades: Mentor Program Fails to Raise Most Pupils' Performance." In response to this disappointment, the Milwaukee
business community withdrew funding for the program's field
staff positions.[1]

In Washington, a year after her original SOS, Dorothy
Gilliam issued another column in the *Washington Post*. This piece,
"Mentoring Has Its Limitations," states, "There is, in my view,
a dangerous trend to look at mentoring as the be-all and end-
all, as the solution to a social ill, as *the* answer to so-called 'at-
risk' youth." Gilliam's perspective came not only from observing the climate now surrounding mentoring and the claims she
heard at the conference, but from her own experience with the
SOS program, which had taught her "the limitations of mentoring." To Gilliam, "Circumstances in some teenagers' lives made
it difficult for them to accept our outreach. . . . Some of us expected too much. Some matches were instant successes, but
others took time and patience just to develop trust."

A year earlier, she had written about thousands of youth
at a crossroads. Now she described mentoring itself "at a crossroads." Warning that mentoring is being oversold, the columnist concluded, "It can either blossom into a useful social tool
or, like a comet that crosses the social scene, plummet and die."[2]

Less Fervor, More Infrastructure

Mentoring represents a unique opportunity because of its gift
for grabbing people's attention — including adults beyond those
traditionally interested in the circumstances of disadvantaged
youth — and directing it toward the provision of a potentially useful service for such youngsters. It may be just as much a "master
key" for reaching adults as youth.

The principal challenge facing the incipient mentoring
movement, one essential for its development and survival, lies
in finding an alternative route, one that might be called fervor
with infrastructure. Taking this route will require a balancing
act that modulates fervor while bolstering infrastructure to strike
the healthy equilibrium between marketing and programming
so lacking at present, and so essential for mentoring to flourish.

Modulating Fervor

Achieving this balance will require less fervor and a different kind of fervor. We need to shed the heroic view of mentoring, one built on the presumption that good-hearted adults can waltz in and quickly change the lives of at-risk youth. Instead of envisioning a cadre of supermentors, Bozzy Hettleman, head of the Baltimore Mentoring Institute, advises planning for average people, and accepting that mentoring with real people will not produce automatic results. It will require care, time, resources, and a tolerance for ambiguity and failure.

Mentoring is mostly about small victories and subtle changes. The marketers of mentoring need to reflect this new perspective, advertising mentoring's ability to help some youth in some ways, and emphasizing the profound commitment that mentoring requires. Enunciating this realism, the National Mentoring Working Group, a group of mentoring practitioners, states, "Mentoring—which is a popular idea at the moment—must not be seen as a cheap fix or a substitute for funding of social services, nor as a primary tool for repairing society's ills."[3]

Mentoring might well be looking for a few good men and women, especially at this stage of the game. It is particularly necessary to jettison the goal of dramatic numbers that has been so dominant in the mentoring field. The push for a million new mentors, a mentor for every youth, is counter-productive in the extreme. First, it is unrealistic to believe that such a large number of people prepared to mentor seriously are going to appear; second, actually achieving this goal might be even more distressing. No structure exists to match, supervise, and support these mentors. Most likely, they would be thrown at kids in an approach that Shayne Schneider likens to "blind dating as social policy."

In place of the big numbers game, the goal must be shifted to one of quality and balance. The mentoring movement is best served by careful and responsible growth, given the continuing scarcity of program funding and the difficulty of the enterprise.

Bolstering Infrastructure

To close the gap between rhetoric and reality, the National Mentoring Working Group urges not only more sober expectations, but more responsible programming. They call for developing what one member calls the art of mentoring for taking seriously the delivery of services. This critical and growing interest in quality mentoring is being encouraged through a proliferation of manuals, conferences, and practitioner networks, a set of supports that comes none too soon.[4]

Reliable knowledge about how and why mentoring works is still at least a few years away, but some common-sense wisdom about the best practices for both mentors and programs is slowly beginning to emerge. The following recommendations are drawn from observations of program and volunteer trial-and-error, the few shards of in-depth research that currently exist, and the distillation of insights presented in the new manuals.

Mentoring Isn't for All Youth. The experiences of mentoring programs strongly suggest that it is much more difficult to serve youth on the edge than good students in need of enrichment, and that efforts must be designed with the difference in mind. If mentoring programs want to serve the most disadvantaged, they must start early and plan to stick around for a long time. Once the "culture of refusal" has taken hold, it is very difficult to connect with young people. Programs must also be prepared to intervene when problems arise and must expect failures and frustrations. As John Hogan points out, many of these young people simply will be unwilling or unable to reach out.

In recognition of these issues, Project RAISE in Baltimore was designed as a six-year program beginning with sixth-graders. However, by the time the second round of RAISE was being planned, program officials were convinced that beginning in the sixth grade was already too late for helping young people who are both living in depressed neighborhoods and struggling in school. RAISE II begins working with youngsters in the second and third grades, also staying with them for six years.

For these and other reasons, a great many programs have

opted not to serve the most at-risk students. Shayne Schneider of Mentors, Inc. believes that volunteer mentoring is generally not a viable intervention for youth who are most at-risk, that it is simply too weak to make much of a difference in their lives. It is worth noting that programs serving only B and C students and only those who volunteer to participate, such as Mentors, Inc., have found that a great many youth perceived as less at-risk often confront many more obstacles than anticipated, and are in many cases in danger of dropping out of school.

Screening Out, Not Screening In. Just as mentoring is not right for all youth, it is not right for all volunteers. Programs should be careful about the mentors they enlist. As Al Abromovitz explains, he "fell in love with the myth of mentoring" in the first year that he ran the Cleveland Career Beginnings site and pushed for big numbers. People would come to the program "expecting that they're going to save the world . . . and we fed them on that . . . reinforced it."

However, as the program struggled through the first years and many of these individuals dropped out, Abromowitz and his staff shifted away from screening people in to screening them out, letting them know about the harder realities of mentoring from the start so that only those individuals really committed would become involved. According to Abromowitz, "We lost some people — the total number of mentors we could claim in the program went down — but the percentage actually performing went up."

Another alternative strategy to screening out involves offering potential volunteers a variety of routes to helping kids. While Philadelphia Futures uses mentoring as the hook to stimulate interest, the program provides a menu of different ways for adults to become directly involved with youth, including tutoring, role-modeling, providing scholarship support, and other options that are less demanding and intensive than mentoring. The program helps interested adults select the particular role that is most compatible with their personality, interests, and level of commitment.

Considering Race, Class, and Love. Common ethnic and racial ties appear to be an advantage in forging connections as those ties mitigate barriers to trust and provide youth with role models that look like them. However, common ethnic or racial background is no guarantee of success.

In fact, common class backgrounds between mentors and students may be even more important. Several studies of mentoring programs have concluded that the most successful mentors are commonly individuals who have weathered "hard lives," growing up in the same way as the youth, often coming from the same neighborhoods and able to talk to them in their own language.[5] The life experiences of these mentors can provide more accessible and realistic models for the youth.

Despite the importance of race and class commonality, there is virtual consensus among program operators that "love matters most." The adults who become involved because they enjoy spending time with young people, rather than because they feel compelled to save youth from poverty, seem to make the greatest strides.

Finally, in the context of considering race and class, it is important to remember that young people need diverse relationships in order to become healthy, biculturally competent adults. While sometimes more difficult to establish, cross-cultural and cross-class relationships can serve an important function for youth endeavoring to comprehend and navigate the adult world.

Preparing Youth. While mentoring is a familiar concept in the world of middle-class adults, it is often a foreign concept to disadvantaged adolescents. When told that they are being assigned a mentor, many youth are resistant or bewildered. Some undoubtedly wonder "What does this say about me — that I need help? That I am deficient?"

Programs have experienced success by orienting students to the mentoring concept prior to the matchmaking process — working to avoid misconceptions and training young people to make the most of the experience. Some programs go even further, engaging the adolescents being mentored as mentors themselves, pairing them up with local elementary school students.

These so-called "tripartite" programs, exemplified by the

Young Leaders program of Mentors, Inc., in Washington, D.C., have numerous advantages. Not only do they support the elementary school children, they also provide participating adolescents with the experience of being mentors themselves. Furthermore, since many of these programs match adolescents and elementary school children growing up in the same neighborhoods, they can also be seen as community-development strategies.

Scheduling Enough Time Together. There is no substitute for mentors and students logging consistent time together. As Ronald Ferguson finds, "Even though a child may settle for what he can get, a minimum of one interaction per week of at least a few hours in duration seems to be the standard for programs where adults play major supplemental parenting roles."[6] If the goal of the mentoring program is primarily exposure to middle-class role models, more occasional contact may suffice. However, if the objective is a significant relationship, then Ferguson's parameters are best seen as irreducible.

Unfortunately, they are rarely accomplished. Recent research on Big Brothers/Big Sisters suggests that even in this program, which mandates weekly contact, pairs get together on the average of three times a month.

Setting Up Tasks as Scaffolding. One experienced program director states, "It would be wonderful if we could just put these two people together and tell them to relate, but it's not realistic."[7] In her experience, when mentors and mentees have something to do or work on together, it gives them more direction. Tasks can absorb initial nervous energy, provide a basis for conversation between partners, and diffuse the stigma of receiving help.

The key is finding the right task — one that interests both parties. Hamilton and Hamilton argue that the workplace is ideal, but admit that finding the right tasks for early adolescents can be more elusive.[8] While tutoring is often the medium selected, this arrangement can be stultifying, since the parties must stop tutoring in order to converse. In contrast, community service projects such as the collaboration between Boston University and Roxbury Middle School, in which mentors and students work side by side, can provide an environment conducive to interchange.

Supporting Mentors. Although there are differing views among practitioners about the value of up-front training of mentors, most agree that some kind of orientation to adolescence and urban poverty is a good idea. But program operators are unequivocal about the importance of supporting mentors and the consequences of failing to do so. In order to combat the isolation in which much mentoring is conducted, some initiatives have begun organizing self-help groups for mentors to provide each other with emotional support, share experiences, and develop solutions to common difficulties. A problem with these sessions, unfortunately, is that it is difficult to get busy mentors to show up for them.

Mentoring teams, where several adults share the difficult job of mentoring several youths, have also helped reduce isolation in some programs. The team structure is used, for example, by the Washington, D.C. office of Latham and Watkins, a law firm, in its program with Hine Junior High School. As an added advantage, the teams help provide consistency for youth. When one of the adults cannot make it to a scheduled session, the youth can still expect to see one or two of the other mentors on the team.

Staffing Carefully. The most important source of support for mentors is also the most important single ingredient in successful mentoring programs: field staff. These individuals are in contact with the kids, the mentors, school staff, and families. Not surprisingly, in programs where such staff are a full-time presence, the whole effort tends to revolve around them; they are the glue in the mentoring process.

Field staff assume many critical functions, from making sure that people show up, to brokering and interpreting for adults and youth, to serving as mentors to the mentors. In part, these youth workers support youth, often with the advantages of social and physical proximity to the young people. Many come from similar socioeconomic backgrounds and set up shop right in the schools that the young people attend. While some programs try to subsist on volunteer coordination, usually by already overworked school counselors, experience suggests that employing full-time youth workers in this role is a far more effective path.

The Art of Mentoring

The preceding guidelines point to ways in which mentoring programs can be made more responsible and less risky. However, as we work toward developing the art of mentoring, there is also an accumulation of wisdom that suggests there is much mentors themselves can do to improve their chances of connecting with young people.[9]

Listening to Youth. The cardinal rule of mentoring is to listen to youth, a practice that seems to define effective mentors more than any other. As John Hogan states: "We talk so much. We're telling kids this and that. We forget to listen. We forget to ask, 'What do you think? How do you feel?' It's only after we know how they feel and what they think that we can know what to say." His adage is listen first. It is the message delivered repeatedly by young people. And it is the only way adults can understand what young people are up against and where opportunities for developing the relationship reside.

Being "Youth-Driven." In a study of effective patterns of interaction, Melenie Styles and Kristine Morrow find that the most important common denominator in successful matches was the ability of mentors to allow the relationship to be "youth-driven." According to Styles and Morrow, these mentors "waited for youth to lower their defenses and to determine when and how trust would be established," in effect "to signal if, when, and in what way the divulgence of personal problems or challenges would occur — indeed, to define the mentor's role." Mentors who enter the relationship with preconceived ideas about what the areas of focus will be, the ways in which they will help youth, and the subjects to be discussed frequently find themselves facing a brick wall.

Building a Relationship. In all the hurry to make a difference, many mentors can forget to take time to build a relationship, to give credence and weight to the process of establishing a firm connection. This means carefully building trust. It means being patient. Many youth will test mentors to see if they are for real. As a mentor manual prepared by psychologists at the University of Illinois urges, "Be patient and don't give up on her. Let her know you are there and that you intend to stay around in case she needs you. Sticking around when she expects you to give up on her sends the very powerful message that she is worth something and that you care enough about her to be there."

Respecting Boundaries. When mentors ask young people personal questions before a solid relationship has been established, the most common response is silence. Young people will clam up. Styles and Morrow found that youth appear to place "a high premium on having these particular boudaries respected." One states, "Sometimes I tell her a few personal things, you know, if it comes up. But it's not like I . . . keep something from her, because whatever I keep from her [is] stuff that I keep from everybody else." Mentors who do not respect young people's needs for privacy are often quick to alienate their partners.

Being Sensitive to Differences. It is necessary to realize that mentors and youth come from different worlds, a reality even for mentors who may have grown up disadvantaged a generation ago. On one level, this means being aware of the embarrassment a young person might feel about being poor. Even Sean Varner was slow to let John Hogan see his family's dwelling: "I rarely let him come to my house, even now, because I am embarrassed about it, because it's not the house that I want, it's not the house that I would have if I was in charge of it." On another level, it means being aware of the ease with which the mentor's and youth's messages to each other can be distorted by cultural differences.

Focusing on Youth. The issue of the mentor's relation to the youth's family is a tricky one, although in some cases powerful and constructive bonds can develop between mentors and families. However, the experience of most programs suggests it is wiser for mentors to pay respects to parents up-front and then focus on the young person. Most young people in mentoring programs are looking for someone who will be there for them. In fact, they often want an independent outlet from their home situation — a safety valve at times — to talk to about things they'd rather not talk to parents about and to help them negotiate changing relationships with parents at a stage in life when these bonds are being redefined.

Providing Support and Challenge. Successful mentors are consistently there for young people, delivering a sustained message that the young people are important. As one student puts it, "He's just there for me, you know, if I want to talk or something, he's always there." When problems arise, effective mentors resist telling young people what to do and instead work with the youth jointly to address the problem. These mentors are able, eventually, to strike a constructive balance between challenge and support — both nurturing youth and pushing them toward their goals.

Acknowledging Reciprocity. While mentors often have to provide all the initiative early in the relationship as trust is being established and the relationship built, mentoring is a two-way street. Growth, benefits, and struggles are present on both sides, and mentors who are able to convey to youth that they are there for mutual exchange — not to solve the problems of the youth — stand the greatest chance of making a solid connection.

Being Realistic. Few mentors turn lives around, but mentors who work with young people toward achievable goals can make a real contribution. Oftentimes this means having a thick skin — tolerating unreturned phone calls, accepting the vicissitudes of adolescence, recognizing the social and cultural gaps that must be bridged. In the end, few virtues in mentoring rival ongoing commitment and genuine caring.

Toward a More Solid Movement

The guidelines in this chapter are designed to strengthen mentoring at both the relationship and the program level. However, there is a third level of infrastructure, which is institutional in nature.

Having wise mentors and sound programs is insufficient if those efforts cannot sustain themselves over time. As Flaxman and Ascher state after reviewing programs for the Ford Foundation, the mentoring field is severely lacking in institutional infrastructure: "Our experience with the high rate of discontinued program telephone numbers, changed addresses, and no answers after a number of calls all testifies to the fluidity of the mentoring programs in New York."[10] This institutional backing is imperative for ensuring quality of service delivery over time, building a track record of reliability, and developing ongoing sources of funding.

As the mentoring movement seeks to become better established, two superb models exist for sustaining one-to-one efforts over time. The first, of course, is Big Brothers/Big Sisters, and it is a private effort. Even though the mentoring movement grew up partly in response to perceived failures of this established effort to meet the needs of disadvantaged youth and to do so on a larger scale, mentoring can learn a great deal from Big Brothers/Big Sisters about delivering quality programming consistently over the decades. As a recent research report argues, Big Brothers/Big Sisters "sets a high standard and offers important lessons for all programs that seek to establish relationships between youth and unrelated adults."

The other model for mentoring, less well known, is the Foster Grandparent program, arguably the largest one-to-one program in the country. In 1990, Foster Grandparents worked with seventy-seven thousand children and youth, most of them disadvantaged, and with twenty-seven thousand Foster Grandparents who provided twenty-eight million hours of service during that year. A War on Poverty program, Foster Grandparents matches low-income Americans over the age of sixty with young people. This program, run by the federal agency ACTION, reveals the important enabling role that government can play in sponsoring voluntarism.

Mentoring will need to borrow from a variety of sources as it seeks to establish and sustain its efforts. Whatever form this movement eventually takes, the basic lesson that continues to resonate is that there is no substitute for infrastructure. Without it, all that remains is fervor. And fervor alone is not only evanescent and insufficient but potentially treacherous.

Answering the Call

Armand Waters is a youth specialist in the One-on-One program in Milwaukee.

You have forty kids and all of them are vying for the attention of the youth specialist. You're a Big Brother, a friend, a counselor, an advocate, a mediator, a doctor. And they reach out to you and a lot of times, you have to kind of step back, and look at the situation, and really ask yourself, am I qualified to help this child, because there is so much need.

And I think one of the most important things to recognize is that these young people trust no one because everything that has been given to them has been taken away. When you go into this child's life and you ask this child to trust you and allow you to help them, they are often leery. Too many times the child's dreams and hopes have been shattered by adults, by the system. It's tricky, and you really have to be genuine. You've got to play sometimes, you've got to be a kid sometimes, you've got to be flexible. Sometimes you're going to cry, and I have felt all of those emotions during the time that I have worked with these kids.

It's just so important that these young people have a chance. All too often, our approach is just to lock them up, they don't get an education, they get put in prison—that doesn't help anything. That's like getting a cut on your hand and when it becomes infected taking a glove and putting it on to hide it. But it's going to rot. Soon you have an infected arm and eventually, you're going to die. I have two children and I wouldn't want anyone to treat mine like that.

We take things a step at a time. If we are able to inspire a child to come to school, be respectful, not get into fights, curse out teachers and whatever, then the next step is to try working on the grades. We try to make them feel comfortable with school, to give

106

them something good each day, to tell them, "Hey you did a wonderful job today, that's a fantastic grade you got, wow." And kids like that, and will respond. We all like to be nurtured—to be recognized—and children are no different.

I grew up in Chicago, and when I was coming up there was a different moral character in the community. Parents were involved with what the children were doing, teachers were involved with the parents, there was a rapport. The neighborhoods were just that, neighborhoods, like a family, though not related by blood. We don't have that now. I live in a community where I don't even know the people across the street, or next door to me, and that did not exist a few years ago.

Volunteer mentors are in a position to assist—I think that should be the operative word, assist, in helping to mold the character of an individual student. I do not believe that a mentor alone, spending a couple of hours a week, or a couple of hours every two weeks, can be everything that the students I work with need. I do believe that mentoring adds another element to that child knowing or experiencing life.

But I think because so many of these kids we deal with are from single-parent families, more often than not from fatherless homes, they need more. Their mother is out trying to be the breadwinner for this child and generally two or three siblings. And she does not have enough time to fully invest in the nurturing process. The youth specialists help with that responsibility. We are here every day.

A mentor is a help to us, as well as a help to the child. But children need more than just someone to look up to and say, "Oh, wow, this guy's fantastic, he took me out and bought me a hot dog and a Coke." They need someone who is like a parent, who can make that kind of investment in the child.

These children also need to see something closer to their reality. Randy [another youth specialist] is the best mentor these kids can have. Why? Because he came up in the same neighborhood as the kids, because he's just like they are, or he was just like they are.

107

Randy can show them, in reality, how to get from point A to point B to point C to point D, because he had to do it himself.

And when he goes into one of the kids' homes and see that it's nasty and it's dirty and that this kid has come to school and his ears are dirty or that his hair isn't combed or that he has a little body odor, he doesn't want to push him off to the side. He wants to take him off to the side and sit him down and explain to him about how to take care of his hygiene, how to deal with these problems. He knows how to go into their home, and whether he has on a shirt and tie, he knows how to go in and sit down and be comfortable.

We get involved with these kids, do everything that we can and sometimes it means burning the midnight oils, sometimes, you know, the school closes at 2:40, and when you leave there at 5:00, you're putting the kid in your car and you're taking the kid home or you're stopping at McDonald's to buy the kid a hamburger and just sit and talk for a few minutes. Or on a Saturday morning the phone rings and you go to the kid's house to talk to the parents. You have students who are not a part of your program that come to you and need help and you say, "Well I've already got forty kids." But then you just can't turn your back, either.

108

8

Closing the Caring Gap

It takes an entire village to raise a child.
—African Proverb

Closing the gap between fervor and infrastructure will help mentors and programs better address disadvantaged youth's need for adult contact and strengthen the support available to adults who provide that contact. However, it would be a mistake either to underestimate the nature of these needs or to overestimate the power of voluntary efforts to meet them. As one program operator warns, "You're not going to have enough mentors. It's not going to work for a lot of kids. There will be a huge hole."

This hole will continue to exist, even if those pushing for responsible volunteer mentoring prevail, because the isolation of youth is a structural problem resulting from a set of fundamental changes in our society. Families and neighborhoods supply few adult supports for youth, and schools and other institutions are not effectively compensating for this deficiency. As these institutions are ever more squeezed for resources, their inadequacies particularly affect disadvantaged children and youth.

Proposing to solve a structural problem of this magnitude through the good will and kindness of volunteers, particularly middle-class professionals already overburdened by their own work and family commitments, is not realistic. Add on the heroic expectations so often attached to mentoring, and the condition moves from unrealistic to treacherous at both the individual and policy levels.

Rather than thinking of volunteer mentoring as a sufficient solution to the problem of youth isolation — particularly a "low-cost, high-yield" one — we would do well to think of the mentoring movement as a potentially important step in the right direction, one that highlights an unmet need, goes part of the way toward redressing it, and calls out for reinforcements.

It is important to be clear about the unmet need that mentoring both highlights and addresses. Most young people growing up in poverty are not "little managers" who simply require some strategic advice, a role model, a few networking opportunities. Few are even in Sean Varner's position, poised to embrace and make catalytic use of intervention by a gifted mentor. A great many young people require support that is developmental, nurturing, protective, and extensive in nature — in other words, something resembling supplemental parenting. They need this caring not only to survive emotionally under adverse conditions but to make the basic transition to adulthood. The role of parents in this struggle is obviously primary, and we need to strengthen support for these adults in their parenting duties. However, as sociologist Joyce Ladner remarks, given the stressful circumstances so many inner-city youth face, most could use three or four parents.

The rise of mentoring reminds us that there is a role for unrelated adults in this process and challenges us to deploy volunteer mentors in a manner that will complement and enhance the family. However, mentoring's rise challenges us to go further, to think of the role other unrelated adults — beyond middle-class volunteers — can play in supporting disadvantaged children.

The Caring Context

Angela Blackwell grew up in St. Louis, in an economically integrated black neighborhood, in the 1950s. She recalls an environment that felt "safe," not just physically but emotionally. It was a neighborhood permeated by the virtues of relationship and responsibility, by a strong feeling of extended kinship.

According to Blackwell, who has spearheaded mentoring efforts in Oakland, mentoring is a proxy for the climate she remembers as a child. Although she admits it is "a weak and artificial proxy," she sees it as a way station in the larger enterprise of reinventing the developmental infrastructure — the village in the African proverb — that she experienced as a youth.

While Blackwell is clear that it is not possible to replace a village with a volunteer, she suggests that we should be thinking of mentoring as an approach to helping young people — a set of principles that needs to be carried further, in new and innovative ways. The mentoring approach can best be advanced by creating more opportunities for young people to interact in their daily lives with an array of caring adults — through creating mentor-rich environments. We will need to fill these environments not only with volunteer mentors from the middle class, who constitute one link in what might be called the continuous chain of caring, but also with teachers, coaches, supervisors, neighbors, youth workers, counselors, social workers, and others with the time and inclination to establish close ties with young people.[1] Creating mentor-rich settings — schools, social programs, youth organizations — is one way of moving beyond the chimera of *supermentoring*, in which a single charismatic adult is called on to be a dramatic influence, providing all the young person's need in one relationship. In reality, young people need more than one relationship to develop into healthy adults.

Young people exposed to mentor-rich settings are in a position to avoid many of the vicissitudes of formal, matched, volunteer mentoring. Rather than being assigned an adult and instructed to form a one-to-one bond with this elder, young people in mentor-rich environments would find ample opportunities for natural connections to develop. In such settings, young people are in a position to select the right mentor at the right time, pick mentors for different reasons, and experience aspects of mentoring from a variety of sources. In the process, these youth might encounter a mix of primary and secondary relationships, with some providing the "master key" and others affording discrete types of help. Some mentors might be of the same race and class, while others might be from different ethnic and socioeconomic groups. The vision presented here is of young people exposed to a variety of caring adult relationships over time. It stands to reason that harder-to-reach youth might particularly benefit from these settings, where there would be many more opportunities to establish trust naturally on a daily basis.

In contrast to the heroic conception of mentoring, the vision articulated here is more organic. It is based on the way mentoring happens in the natural world — not through formal matches but through informal interaction. Our aspiration should be to create planned environments conducive to the kind of informal interaction that leads to mentoring. Indeed, such an approach is rooted in the historic strength and traditional practice of extended and fictive kin structures in many low-income communities — particularly African-American neighborhoods.

Despite such advantages, there can be no question about the difficulty of this undertaking. As Nathan Glazer argues, while reconstructing the "fine structure of society" is now one of the most important tasks confronting social policy, it is far "easier to recognize these needs symbolically than to do something about them in concrete policy."[2]

The New Heads

In moving from the symbolic to the concrete, mentoring programs themselves provide essential clues about how to proceed. The most important of these clues come from their field staff, many of whom form powerful mentoring relationships with participating youth. Erik Butler, who was instrumental in the design and direction of Career Beginnings, points out that "in a lot of Career Beginnings programs, the primary relationships are between the case managers and the kids, and only secondarily and maybe supportively between the [volunteer] mentors and the kids."

Butler's position is echoed by Harvard's Ronald Ferguson, whose examination of community-based programs for young black males provided a similar perspective. According to Ferguson, the mentors in the programs he studied are "sometimes volunteers, but more often they are paid staff members who teach, broker resources, and provide supplemental parenting in what they characterize frequently as 'love' and 'extended-family' relationships."[3]

This insight comes also from the I Have a Dream project, where one analyst writes that the most essential function of the project coordinator role is as mentor to the students. He adds that this figure has *sustained and comprehensive involvement* with the students in the program, functioning "more like a parent, aunt or uncle, or an older sibling than like a bureaucrat." An *Education Week* article describes these I Have a Dream youth workers as being "like guardian angels who provide the daily guidance and support needed to make sure the students have a shot at collecting on their sponsor's tuition offer."[4]

In this way, volunteer mentoring programs — as well as efforts like I Have a Dream — end up serving as back doors to traditional youth work; the need to administer the program serves as justification for hiring adult staff who themselves come to provide the most critical mentoring delivered by the program. Back door or not, the role many staff come to play underscores the basic insight that mentoring, while cast as voluntary relationship, is by no means the exclusive province of volunteers.

Indeed, these youth workers are generally in a much better position than volunteers to connect with young people. First, they are on hand, present five days a week, in close physical proximity. When troubles arise in youths' lives, the project coordinator is not away on a business trip or even downtown in an office building. They can attend to the issue immediately. Second, these individuals are in a position to provide continuity of caring to youth, usually extending well beyond the duration of volunteer mentors, enabling them to stick with youth through institutional and developmental transitions. In I Have a Dream, coordinators are hired with the understanding that they will remain in place for six years.

The third, and perhaps most important, asset of the coordinators is their social proximity. These youth workers tend to be individuals who have "come up" in the same way as the youth, and who often continue to live in the neighborhood where the program is located. As a result, they are much more easily integrated into the young person's natural networks.

The individuals who come forward to fill these youth worker positions tend to combine the full-time, formal presence of a professional social worker, with the sense of mission often associated with volunteers. Their role, with its focus on the provision of relationships, is unique in the context of the schools and social programs where they set up shop. As a result, these individuals are frequently overwhelmed by need as they become established and trusted. Young people flood their offices in search of someone to talk to or help them out.

In their strong focus on nurturance and socialization, these youth workers are the authentic heirs to the "old heads" Elijah Anderson describes. Many of these individuals had their own lives shaped by such figures in their youth and see this work as an opportunity to pass on what they've received. As Aaron Conner, a project coordinator in RAISE, states, "Basically, I have a love and interest in working with youth, and I have a vested interest in the black community. I want to give back to the young people the kind of thing I've gotten out of people telling me, when I was coming up, 'you can make it.'"

Individuals like Conner and Armand Waters are appearing in a wide variety of community programs, not just mentoring efforts and initiatives like I Have a Dream but in Afrocentric programs, antigang efforts, youth organizations, church-sponsored efforts, and more traditional outlets like Boys and Girls Clubs. Their emergence reflects, to some extent, the resilience of inner-city neighborhoods, which continue to possess many individuals committed to the ethic of responsibility and decency. However, this resilience is increasingly precarious. In *Streetwise,* Anderson quotes Tyrone Pitts, an "old head" who is working to help youth in Northton, to illustrate this point: "We are the last line of defense. After this there's pure death [for our community]. That's why we don't mind stepping into the teeth of it. If we don't do that, then there is no hope for anything else."[5]

Duneier's research on the men who gather at Slim's table implies that there are many potential Tyrone Pittses in America's inner cities who might be lured back to roles involved in nurturing, developing, and socializing young people if better mechanisms existed for them to get involved. The natural vehicles are no longer there. In the absence of such mechanisms, a few particularly dedicated individuals will still find a way to become involved, but most will simply abstain.

In recognition of the need for new mechanisms, David Liederman, executive director of the Child Welfare League of America, calls for establishment of a corps of inner-city youth workers, "able to hit the streets and work directly with kids in their own neighborhoods." He argues that our young people desperately need caring adult models they can "see, touch, and talk to," not just famous athletes or television stars who deliver inspirational messages. Envisioning a "small army of trained, committed youth workers talking about and developing positive values, keeping kids in school and helping them get decent jobs," Liederman argues that these individuals would not only constitute a strong, stabilizing force in neighborhoods but also "be there when the kids need them."

Along with working toward the creation of new structures like Liederman's corps notion, we would be well advised also to strengthen the range of community organizations serving youth. This means bolstering the growing number of grassroots youth organizations that have sprung up around the country while also adapting the efforts of the more traditional youth-serving organizations to better help low-income neighborhoods.

In pursuing a broader neighborhood strategy focused on providing more adult-youth relationship opportunities and particularly on creating mechanisms bringing indigenous adults together with young people, mentoring programs themselves might widen their recruitment efforts to go after not only successful role models from the professional class but also adults who live in the same neighborhoods as youth.

Finally, enormous promise resides in the involvement of youth themselves, through efforts enabling older adolescents to work with early adolescents or neighborhood children. These peer programs show considerable potential not only for adding support to the lives of the younger kids but for simultaneously stimulating the development of the older students.

School Reform

The quest to provide mentor-rich environments for youth leads logically to the realm of institutions, most prominently to the reform of public schools. In the past, these institutions were one of the most important sources of adult mentors for youth, and today youth spend more time in school than in any other single setting.

Through numerous pragmatic suggestions, a growing number of policymakers, researchers, and practitioners have recognized the need "to build into our schools and other institutions that deal with young people a quality of caring, a friendly climate that makes them feel wanted, appreciated, and valued as individuals."[6]

The most straightforward recommendations focus on cutting student-counselor and student-teacher ratios. One strategy to improve the student-counselor ratio is on view in the Los Angeles public schools. The Focus on Youth program, privately funded by ARCO, concentrates on 150 marginal students in each of thirteen inner-city middle and high schools with high absentee rates, low grades, and major behavior problems. Each counselor in the program becomes intensively involved with their students, each day asking, "Are you here? Are you clean? Have you eaten? Do you have books, paper, eyeglasses?" while driving home the message, "I care." The counselors in the program are instructed that their first responsibility is to the students, to advocate on their behalves as parents might.[7]

With the objective of enabling teachers to have more sustained and individualized contact with students, Theodore Sizer of Brown University suggests that by changing assignments and the way teachers work with each other, the pupil-teacher ratio can be cut dramatically. Instead of seeing 150 different students a day, teachers can have their loads cut to 80 students daily—still not ideal, but a vast improvement.

James Garbarino makes the case for school reforms that take into account the needs of young people confronting enormous violence and stress. Arguing for a renewed appreciation of the role of the schools as safe harbors for youth emphasizing "the importance of close, mutually reinforcing, and growth-enhancing relationships between adults and children," Garbarino and his colleagues propose two measures designed to enhance adult-youth relationships.

Garbarino's plan is based on the use of subgrouping and of a figure he calls the *attachment teacher*. In this proposal, each classroom is divided into subgroups of six or seven students, which have an actual physical location that serves as a home base from which children can venture forth into the larger, more challenging social environment of the classroom. Each subgroup functions like a family, with its own events, celebrations, routines, and history. Furthermore, each subgroup has an attachment teacher, an adult whose primary responsibility is to develop close relationships with a small group of children. The bonds are designed to provide a secure base for the childrens' affective and cognitive development. The attachment teacher is never reassigned to another group, nor interchanged to another group during the day. She provides one of the most essential, and often missing, features in the life of kids and of schools: continuity of caring.[8]

One of the most sweeping visions of relationship-focused school reform comes from the Carnegie Council on Adolescent Development, through its *Turning Points* report aimed at transforming the country's middle schools. The council's study advocates the creation of communities of learning in these middle schools, based on a three-tiered plan: cutting schools down into smaller units; engaging youth and adults in teams; and instituting one-to-one adviser systems. Carnegie Corporation President David Hamburg states: "The transformed middle school would provide time and a structure for teachers and other professional staff to become mentors and advocates for students."[9]

The Common Denominator

Drawing on his own experience, one seventeen-year-old participant in Project Roadmap in Baltimore — an effort infused with mentoring — explains why these relationships are so important:

The [other programs for high school dropouts] didn't work. That's why I'm here now. This program has been the best so far. People ask me what's so special about this program. It's the people. They care and they deliver. Whereas the other programs they never put their personal feelings in it; it was just like a nine-to-five type thing. Here, it's the counselors, the mentors, everybody involved in the program . . . they want to help you . . . it's real. [There's] nothing false about it. You just get a feel for what's real and what's not real — these people are in it with their heart.[10]

Researchers studying schools and social programs provide considerable evidence to support this firsthand perspective, suggesting that it is precisely these institutions, the kind that are adept at fostering bonds between adults and youth — that are able to create environments encouraging relationships, personal attention, and caring — that have the best track records in helping youth. In other words, the principles of mentoring may well be among the most important common denominators across effective programs for disadvantaged youth. In the words of Erwin Flaxman of the Institute of Urban and Minority Education at Columbia University, mentoring may amount to the "DNA" in successful youth programming.

Indeed, these familylike environments seem to be the active ingredient in a wide array of effective schools and social programs. These are all initiatives where, in the words of the Hispanic Policy Development Project, "caring had been institutionalized as a value . . . and not solely an accidental relationship between a teacher and a lucky student."[11] Five examples of this research reflect a much broader body.

In *Adolescents At-Risk,* Joy Dryfoos analyzes over one hundred successful programs for at-risk youth, concluding that a distinguishing feature of these interventions is that "each child can count on at least one adult who has the responsibility and resources to support him," citing "very strong evidence that without such support most high-risk children will not be able to move ahead."[12]

Studying effective schools for disadvantaged youth, Mihaly Csikszentmihalyi and Jane McCormack of the University of Chicago set out to learn what "distinguishes teachers who, despite all the obstacles, are able to touch students' lives?" Their answer is the qualities of relationship and caring: "Teenagers saw nurturance as important because, in one teenager's words, 'It shows you that the teacher really cares, and just seeing that makes *you* want to learn.'"[13]

Harvard education professor Sara Lawrence Lightfoot writes in *The Good High School* that all six effective institutions she studied shared an emphasis on relationship reinforced by their leaders: "The schools had very different leaders. But one quality all of the leaders shared was their focus on nurturance. . . . They are people who orchestrate relationships. . . . They talked about listening, building a sense of community, sustaining relationships, and supporting people through failure."[14]

Anthony Bryk and Mary Driscoll of the University of Chicago, in their study of effective schools, find the primary importance of "an ethos of caring, manifested particularly in teachers' willingness to extend their roles beyond classroom teaching."[15]

The recurring emphasis placed on personal attention, caring, and connection in these research findings is stressed as well in a recent study by the Institute for Education in Transformation of the Claremont Graduate School, which identifies a profound disjuncture between the remedies offered by most education reformers and the critical issues identified by students, teachers, and parents. Indeed, the researchers themselves were stunned by their findings: "No one was more surprised by the results of this report than those of us on the outside. We, like the authors of previous reports on schooling and teacher education, would have predicted issues such as what to teach, how to measure it, how much a teacher knows, and choice of school would have surfaced." However, these were not the issues that arose.

What surfaced, in a word, was relationships. According to John Maguire, president of Claremont University, "If the relationships are wrong" in the school, particularly between adults and youth, "you can restructure until the cows come home, but transformation won't take place." The report quotes one principal who describes the school day as "nothing more than a series of relationships." According to a middle-school teacher surveyed, "We have to put relationships at the core of what we're doing." The study concludes, however, that despite a considerable body of research pointing to the centrality of personal connection in effective education, schools in general are terrible at relationships, contributing to "a pervasive sense of despair" in American education today.[16]

Another Crossroads

These instances of interest in personalizing the settings where young people spend their time constitute welcome news. But these signs only point out the road ahead. Getting any distance down that road will be a formidable challenge. The first requirement will be new thinking about how best to foster nurturing relationships for youth — thinking that must surmount the impulse to segregate caring functions exclusively in specialized positions like that of the school counselor or volunteers. However, the most formidable challenge will be not in the realm of thinking but that of finding hard cash.

One of the best illustrations of this challenge is offered by adviser systems, like those advocated by the Carnegie Council. As school principal Thomas Edwards points out, structural measures such as advisers cost money: "If . . . public school teachers are already overburdened with teaching loads and institutional requirements, where can they find the time to take on new responsibilities?" The answer is, they can't and this is the biggest reason the vast majority of advisory systems are located in wealthy school districts. In order to advise a student, Edwards continues, "more teachers would have to be hired to teach the sections left uncovered as staff members devote time to advising. . . . Thus, economics hinders the spread of advising systems in public schools."[17]

As awareness grows about the importance of adult relationships for youth in the settings increasingly entrusted with their education, nurturance, and development, we continue to undercut their ability to provide such support. If anything, we are moving in the opposite direction: cutting staff, clearing away all but the most essential roles, burdening the remaining adults with so many formal responsibilities that forming relationships with struggling young people, or bringing in volunteers to do so, becomes a virtual impossibility.

A compelling irony of the new mentoring movement is that this strategy, pursued by many as a cheap fix, not only costs money to do responsibly but leads logically to a set of reforms that are among the most costly imaginable. Valuing human resources is expensive; any doubt about that connection is quickly dispelled by calculating the cost of reducing student-teacher ratios. These costs are currently beyond our political will to pay.[18]

So we, as a society, face a choice. We can continue to pin our hopes on purely voluntarist strategies to provide the personal attention so badly needed by our young, particularly those growing up in poverty. Or we can view voluntary mentoring as a starting point, one step in a necessary set of humanizing reforms that will make our schools, social programs, and inner-city neighborhoods better places for American youth.

Should we choose to cling to voluntarism as our principal strategy, we must at least be willing to acknowledge that we are not likely to lessen the profound isolation of our young people in anything but a modest and glancing fashion. This admission will have the advantage not only of honesty but of freeing mentoring from the burden of expectation that it can never realistically fulfill.

people have their jaundiced view and their prejudice—I've got to be
careful, I don't want to indict a whole class—but I mean people have
their long-term, cemented view of certain things. And when you can
sit across from somebody at a dinner party and say, "You know,
you're really not right, you really aren't. This is really what people go
through and let me tell you about this working mother and what she
goes through every day and how she works twice as hard as you and
I ever thought about working. And then what's her reward in life?"
And you have to change people's mind-sets, and hopefully we're
changing our children's mind-sets through this whole thing. And now
I'm starting to sound altruistic, but I mean that's the reality, we've
got to change the way we think about these kinds of things.

If enough of us continue to speak up as a whole then maybe
we can make a little bit of difference in the system. If not, then we're
just sand on the beach, you know, pebbles in the ocean.

9

Reengaging the Middle Class

If one man dies, it is a tragedy;
if a thousand men die, it is a statistic.
—Phillipe Berthelot

*W*hile meeting the needs of youth for caring adult contact will require moving beyond the sphere of voluntarism, it is essential that volunteer mentoring itself—and the wider notion of middle-class engagement with disadvantaged youth—not be lost in the quest to enact a broader set of humanizing reforms. Why should we make an effort to preserve volunteer involvement—given that doing so responsibly will cost money and entail some risks? Part of the reason is that volunteers can provide direct help to youth; there is a place for them in the village that must be constructed around our most vulnerable young people.

A second reason for maintaining volunteer involvement is mentoring's potential for meeting important needs of adults, who can benefit themselves from the mentoring interaction, through satisfying a sense of generativity. Mentoring is a reciprocal relationship. As Charles Healy and Alice Welchert write, mutual exchange is the "sine qua non of mentoring."[1]

Yet there is another reason for pursuing the volunteer wing of mentoring that extends beyond the direct help mentors can provide to youth and the emotional benefits to be reaped by these adults in the process. Mentoring is not only about combating the isolation pervasive *within* low-income communities but also about bridging the chasm that exists between these communities and the mainstream of American life. As such it offers a vehicle for breaking through the "innocence" of the middle class to which Dorothy Gilliam referred in her SOS and constitutes an opportunity to begin mobilizing our dormant public will. Without this will, there can be little hope for any substantial reforms aimed at ameliorating the conditions of young people in poverty and the institutions that serve them.

Two Nations

Writing of England in 1845, Benjamin Disraeli described social divisions so deeply etched that his country had, in effect, split into two nations between whom there was "no intercourse and no sympathy; who are as ignorant of each other's habits, thought, and feelings, as if they were dwellers in different zones, or inhabitants of different planets."[2]

One hundred and fifty years later, in this country, Disraeli's description carries an eerie and familiar ring. Part of the social gulf in America today is economic. Inequity of income and wealth has widened dramatically since the late 1970s. The top 20 percent of Americans—the group Robert Reich calls "the fortunate fifth"—now earn 47 percent of the country's total income, while the bottom fifth makes just 3.9 percent. By 1992, following a decade when the after-tax income of the top one percent of society rose a stunning 77 percent, the U.S. government reported that American poverty had reached the highest levels since 1964.[3]

But economic inequality, even numbers as stark as these, leave part of our "two nations" story untold. The great chasm that exists today is as much social as economic; as Nicholas Lemann states, ever since "the riots of the 1960s, a quite elaborate social reorganization of American metropolitan life has taken place based on the principle of everybody getting as far away from the underclass as possible."[4] After the riots of 1992, it is reasonable to fear that this evacuation is only accelerating.

The 1990 census confirms for the first time that more Americans live in the suburbs than anywhere else. Increasingly these individuals no longer work in urban America either, as many corporations locate outside the central cities. Furthermore, as James Fallows observes, the vast structures that once provided contact between the poor and nonpoor, "the institutions that kept Americans in contact with one another — the public schools, the 'general' publications, the middle-class army," have all eroded badly over the past generation.[5]

Indeed, the poor in America are so cut off — and so badly off — that the Peace Corps has begun preparing volunteers for service in distant Third World countries by exposing them to inner-city America. One location where this is occurring is Camden, New Jersey, which has the highest percentage of children living in poverty — 65 percent — of any city in the United States. Following training at a Camden elementary school, one volunteer states, "The situation is very similar in many ways to the Third World. . . . I think it will lessen the shock for us." Another admits, "I had no idea that things could be this bad in this country."[6]

Without contact between the classes, fear and misunderstanding grow. As Alex Kotlowitz illustrates in *There Are No Children Here,* these perceptions exist in grotesque proportions on both sides of the great social divide. In his book, Kotlowitz recounts an incident near railroad tracks running by the Henry Horner housing project in Chicago, where Lafeyette and Pharoah Rivers, the two boys whose lives he chronicles, are playing. Along with friends they are standing next to an empty boxcar, when a commuter train is sighted approaching from downtown. One of the boys yells, "There's a train!"

> James frantically helped Lafeyette climb into the open boxcar, where they found refuge in a dark corner. Others hid behind the boxcar's huge wheels. Pharoah and Porkchop threw themselves headlong

into the weeds, where they lay motionless on their bellies. "Keep quiet," came a voice from the thick bushes. "Shut up," another barked.

The youngsters had heard that the suburb-bound commuters, from behind the tinted train windows, would shoot at them for trespassing on the tracks. One of the boys, certain that the commuters were crack shots, burst into tears as the train whisked by.

While no one on the train bursts into tears, there is greater edginess within the cars as they travel by the Henry Horner Homes. Some of the passengers had also heard rumors that the neighborhood's youth would shoot at the trains; they "worried that, like the cardboard lions in a carnival shooting gallery, they might be the target of talented snipers." Some move away from the windows until safely past the projects. Kotlowitz comments that "for both the boys and the commuters, the unknown was the enemy."[7]

Disengagement and Disinvestment

One consequence of the "two nations" is rising mistrust and misunderstanding. Another is disinvestment. As the middle and upper classes exit the cities they take with them social capital. They also take financial capital, in their tax dollars. The result is a country full of urban areas where social problems are spiraling out of control, fiscal resources to deal with them are dwindling, and the immediate impact on most Americans, all the while, is fairly faint.

One consequence of flight is a decreased direct stake in the institutions that serve disadvantaged youth. Indeed, nowhere is disengagement and disinvestment more evident than in the urban public schools, which are reeling in the wake of middle-class exodus. Those who haven't departed for the suburbs send their kids to private or parochial schools. Furthermore, demographic trends, such as the aging of the population, mean that fewer adults in the community have a direct tie to the public schools. Without such a stake, political support withers. And schools are not only forced to make do with less money but lose powerful advocates.

Overall, the poor are becoming more invisible. Out of sight, their troubles remain mostly out of the public mind. Twenty-five years ago, sociologist Philip Slater called this condition "the toilet assumption," the belief that "unwanted matter . . . difficulties . . . complexities . . . will disappear if they're removed from our immediate field of vision."[8] Out of sight, efforts designed to ameliorate these problems will also likely remain out of money. This is particularly true with respect to poor children who can't vote, whose parents tend not to vote, who truly remain orphans at the ballot box.

Indeed this problem of invisibility might well increase in the future. One of the remedies proposed for the current caregiving crisis in low-income neighborhoods is the establishment of new "orphanages" for urban youth. William Bennett, the former Secretary of Education, states, "We may just have to find some way for children to get out of the environment they are in, to go to orphanages, to go to Boys' Towns, to institutions where they will be raised and nurtured."[9]

Direct Contact

Against the backdrop of increasing class isolation come calls for a new awareness of the circumstances of poverty among mainstream Americans. The *New York Times* writes that one of the most important political challenges of the 1990s is finding a way "to summon the national will to address a problem that the nation has done its best to isolate and flee," while sociologist Paul Starr of Princeton states that explaining the stake Americans have in other people's children — particularly the children of the poor — is one of the critical tasks of the current decade.[10]

In this vein, the *Washington Monthly* has argued that we need "a new Dickens" capable of building bridges of understanding between the classes, recalling Daniel Webster's observation that Dickens had "done more to ameliorate the condition of the English poor than all the statesmen Great Britain had sent into

Parliament."[11] While there is certainly precedent for such a role in our recent social history (Michael Harrington's *The Other America* being the most vivid example) and while writers like Kotlowitz are worthy of this noble tradition, many have come to believe that Americans are inured to vicarious accounts of the suffering of the poor.

A recent *Washington Post* report, "Even Madison Avenue Has Trouble Selling Public on Aiding the Poor," details a failed effort by the Ad Council to find an advertising campaign capable of galvanizing support for young people living in poverty. However, the effort did detect promise in projects involving direct contact. The article goes on to quote an official of the Association of Child Advocates, who concludes that for the "community to be mobilized, people have to feel that they can do something themselves."[12]

Coming to a similar conclusion, the Children's Defense Fund states, 'While many people read about the serious difficulties faced by poor children and families, our experience shows that it is often not until individuals can see child suffering and desperation, and feel family struggles for themselves, that they become ready and motivated to work for change."[13] In other words, in today's environment few means short of direct contact appear capable of stirring people's commitment and generating action.

The tradition of direct contact as a vehicle for developing understanding and sympathy toward the poor, essentially the idea of an inverted social program, has a long history in America, the most outstanding example being the century-old settlement house movement. Animated by a desire to "reestablish those social relations which modern city life has thrown into confusion," the settlement houses accomplished little in the way of the reforms they set out to pursue, but their biggest impact was on the procession of young men and women who passed through them, "a group of individuals who were touched indelibly by their brush with poverty, and whose subsequent careers reflected that stamp."

The settlement workers included Julia Lathrop, first chief of the U.S. Children's Bureau; Grace Abbott, who succeeded her; Edith Abbott, founding dean of the University of Chicago School of Social Service Administration; the philosopher and educator John Dewey; Frances Perkins, Secretary of Labor under Franklin Roosevelt; and Harry Hopkins, architect of Roosevelt's federal relief programs, along with many others who went into public service related to the concerns of the poor.[14]

A Social Program for Adults

In this context of disengagement, mentoring offers one of the few opportunities in our society today for bringing adults from the social and economic mainstream into direct contact with disadvantaged youth. In this capacity, mentoring can function as a social program for adults, who are in many respects just as isolated and disconnected as the youth targeted by mentoring programs. Many adults are cut off from school children in a society sharply segregated by age, separated from public life and civic duty in a nation where active citizenship has eroded badly, and protected from poverty in a country ever more sharply divided by class. These mainstream adults are as removed from the reality of poverty as poor children are from the experience of middle-class life.

Sponsors of mentoring programs admit that a central part of their mission is alerting middle-class adults to the circumstances of poor children, and in the process helping to reconstruct a constituency for these young people. Bob Embry, president of the Abell Foundation and founder of Project RAISE, is intent on getting a lot more middle-class adults involved with kids, "because the middle class is, by definition, the group that affects society, in terms of how they spend their money, how they vote, what they ask their local representatives to do or don't do." Embry remarks that urban public schools are no longer "the American ideal where the mill owner's child and the mill worker's child are being educated side by side," and as a result we must find new mechanisms for rebuilding stake.

Marcienne Mattleman, who created the Philadelphia Futures mentoring program, concurs. Mattleman states that while her official goal is motivating kids to stay in school, and while

that objective is certainly important, "what we're really doing
to make that happen is mobilizing public support" for the schools.

Angela Blackwell of the Oakland Urban Strategies Council
envisions mentoring as a way of galvanizing middle-class blacks —
a community already sensitive to racial injustices — to class issues as well: "There is a constituency out there that gets mad
at the governor if he vetoes a piece of civil rights legislation,"
but not a piece of anti-poverty legislation. Blackwell believes that
mentoring may be able "to broaden the view of people to generate
the same outrage when social programs are under attack."

As a program for involving adults, mentoring is built
around the power of direct experience. Decent and caring people, good-hearted people who are nonetheless inured to the realities of poverty, are brought face to face with the unjust manner
in which poverty afflicts innocent children. This approach ac-
cords with psychological research demonstrating that people are
less willing to tolerate suffering in those who can be seen, heard,
and touched, whose humanity is made visible.

The experience of direct contact that mentors describe begins simply by understanding the basic humanity and complexity
of the young person. Mentoring offers a context to experience
and acknowledge that humanity, one not afforded by everyday
street interactions. This contact can often lead to basic social
education.

Lifting the veil of social innocence often leaves the volunteer stunned; like the Peace Corps trainees in Camden, Baltimore mentor Eileen Benton describes feeling a sense of shell
shock: "I'd never really ridden into the city. Not that I come from
an affluent neighborhood; I'm from a modest background, but
I never really wanted for anything. To see what some of these
children have to go through to get a decent pair of shoes, or a
pair of glasses! These aren't frivolous things that they want."

Another mentor in Milwaukee describes taking his student fishing, discovering on the way back that the youngster had
bumps all over his arms. The mentor assumed the bumps were
an allergic reaction to the fish and took the youth to a doctor,
who explained that the bumps were flea bites. This helped the
mentor better understand the troubles the student was having

in school: "Now how does a kid concentrate the next day in school when he's all bitten up with fleas? I know now that these aren't only excuses, they are part of the reality of why that child can't function. And unless we are constantly reminded of these things, we start to lose sight of them."

Like this mentor, many adults describe a realization of how fundamental the needs of these young people are. Even for mentors like Sharon Steiner, long concerned about issues of poverty, direct experience tends to drive home lessons; before working with Rita, Sharon states that she understood poverty's effects "intellectually," while now she understands "emotionally."

Direct contact educates mentors. It serves to correct misconceptions and to develop a more realistic and complicated picture of how disadvantaged young people are living. Beyond education, direct contact is also a route to empathy, and many mentors are moved to wonder how they or their children would respond under similarly difficult circumstances.

Dalton James, an investment banker and mentor in Baltimore, is led to compare his mentee, Lewis, with his own children: "Now with our kids, flip a coin, it always comes out heads in their lives. Lewis is half-and-half, or three-quarters tails, a loser. That's wrong, and it is unrelated to ability or innate motivation." Empathic responses like Dalton James's, fueled by an offended sense of fairness, present an opportunity to build both stake and advocacy.

James, who advocates for Lewis with teachers and the school district, states that the student's troubles are hardly isolated: "Over 60 percent of these kids will drop out of the system and have no opportunity." He states that this constitutes abandonment: "Abandonment is what everybody's doing. They're saying, 'These kids are the dregs of society. Forget them.'" He adds, "At least in this stage of my life, I'm not willing to accept that as an appropriate response anymore. . . . These kids deserve a chance. And they're not getting a chance."

Mentors like James not only come to advocate for their students with the education and social service system, but begin to work at another level as well. Richard Morris's comments, preceding this chapter, provide an example. Morris's pilgrimage from involvement to advocacy has meant that he's not only taken on a series of students to mentor, but has become a strong advocate in the business community for funding mentoring and school reform efforts. He's opened up job opportunities at his television station for young people from the school where he's been involved. Perhaps most significantly, in social settings, he tries to convey his experience and its lessons to friends and acquaintances who harbor prejudices against disadvantaged youth. As Richard says, "If enough of us continue to speak up as a whole we can make a little bit of difference in the system."

The route from direct contact to empathy to stake, described by mentors in every program, raises historian Christopher Lasch's observation that Americans do not maintain abstract affinity well: "The capacity for loyalty is stretched too thin when it tries to attach itself to the hypothetical solidarity of the whole human race. It needs to attach itself to specific people and places."[15]

The experience of mentoring suggests a variant on Lasch's point. Our capacity to take responsibility for strangers and the future, perhaps nowhere better embodied than in disadvantaged youth, is so badly atrophied that it can only be reconstructed by moving from the specific to the general. Anthropologist Mary Catherine Bateson states, "Every adult needs a relationship with a flesh-and-blood child, so that we can imagine what it will be like as that child's life unfolds into the future." For Bateson, we need to return to "the elementary school of caring."[16]

Mentoring amounts to the "elementary school of caring" for other people's children, the children of the poor. It is a specific context in which to initiate the process of reconstructing empathy, and also a platform for the building of advocacy and stake — immediately for specific children, but also more generally for disadvantaged youth.

The Challenge of Reengagement

Patricia Albjerg Graham, president of the Spencer Foundation and former dean of the Harvard Graduate School of Education, argues that, historically, volunteer movements such as mentoring, while unable to provide fundamental reform in and of themselves, have often "set the stage so that fundamental reform becomes more likely." Graham believes these movements are valuable because they build a sense of stake among the enfranchised who come to provide poor children with "new and powerful advocates for the schooling they need."[17] The experience of mentoring suggests much to confirm Graham's perspective. At the same time, some obvious caveats are in order.

First, mentoring is risky. Direct contact is a double-edged sword. This section has highlighted its constructive potential, but as earlier sections contend, direct contact can backfire, reinforcing stereotypes and prompting disengagement.

Second, the barriers of poverty are formidable, and individual outrage at these conditions on the part of mentors can as easily lead to hopelessness as to advocacy. Some mentors find themselves feeling, as already mentioned, "like a drop in the bucket."

Third, large numbers of mentor/advocates are unlikely. The prospect of a mass outcry for change emanating from transformed mentors seems fairly remote.

Fourth, while mentors can develop a sense of stake and contribute to a constituency for youth, being a mentor is not the same as sending your children to the same public schools as the disadvantaged, nor is it the same as living in a settlement house in a low-income neighborhood as so many did during the earlier part of the century.

Nevertheless, there is much promise in mentoring as a vehicle for reengaging *some* adults and of suggesting ways for getting the attention of others. The first step toward meeting the challenge is to meet an earlier one: conducting responsible mentoring. Mentors are much more likely to become reengaged if they are carefully screened, supported, and supervised, and if there is quick intervention on the part of staff when things go wrong. There is no such thing as instant empathy.

The second step is for mentoring programs to be less reticent about functioning as social programs for adults. While these efforts need not advertise themselves as adult initiatives, they could be far more proactive, taking a few lessons from the field of organizing. To start, programs could bring mentors together to share and help make sense of their experiences and to determine ways of acting in concert around issues of strong mutual concern. In particular, these sessions could focus on the often expressed desire of mentors to be part of a broader support network for the young people. Around this desire, mentors could be encouraged to press for the kinds of humanizing changes outlined in the preceding section.

The third step in this challenge actually moves past volunteers to a wider circle of potentially engaged adults. While it is ill-advised to inflate the number of mentors unnaturally, mentoring might profitably be used to stimulate other avenues of direct engagement. The Philadelphia Futures program provides an example of how this potential might be tapped. While Philadelphia Futures uses mentoring as the hook, the program provides a menu of different ways for adults to become directly involved with youth, including tutoring, role-modeling, and other options. The program helps interested adults select the particular role that is most compatible with their personality, interests, and level of commitment.

In other words, with this approach, mentoring is just one way for caring adults to become involved. Without making every interested adult into a mentor, it may well be possible to increase the number who have contact with poor kids, come to understand their needs, have the opportunity to help, and feel an enhanced stake in their fate.

And mentoring efforts are not alone in this enterprise. The past few years have seen a small renaissance of initiatives designed to promote direct contact between middle-class adults and poor children. Nationally, for example, the Children's Defense Fund is introducing the Child Watch Visitation Project in conjunction with six partners: AARP, the Association of Junior Leagues, Kiwanis International, the National Council of La Raza, the National Council of Negro Women, and United Methodist Women, with plans to introduce the model in one hundred cities over a two-year period.

The project focuses on a broad range of community leaders across the country and is designed to educate and involve them in "the variety and extent of child and family need" through a combination of contact with young people, briefings by policy and program experts, and targeted background and policy materials. The goal of the effort is to "personalize child suffering" and through doing so to galvanize a critical mass of concerned and influential citizens.

Another important undertaking, one of great interest from the perspective of building critical mass, is now underway in Atlanta. The Atlanta Project grows out of Jimmy Carter's experience working in the Habitat for Humanity program. Carter was so impressed with the poor people he worked side by side with in the project, and so struck by the misconceptions he and others held, that the former president decided to launch a citywide effort to bring together "rich Atlanta" and "poor Atlanta." According to Carter, "We try, in effect, without even thinking about it, just to associate with people just like us. We don't want to meet strange people. I think when you meet those people, you find they're not very strange. They're just like us. They haven't had a good chance in life."[18]

Carter acknowledges that the class gap can be an almost "impossible chasm for some of us to cross," but is hoping that "with an adequate degree of groundwork and acculturation it can be done." Participants in the Atlanta project serve as mentors, help in day-care centers, volunteer in schools in low-income areas, and work in a variety of settings involving direct contact.

The final challenge of reengagement is to understand more broadly the appeal mentoring holds, for understanding this appeal might provide important clues for social policies and programs that are both saleable and sustainable. At root, the appeal of mentoring is reflected in its essential principles of connection and reciprocity, of relationship and participation. It is reflected as well in the words of mentors who speak of "recreating the extended family," of "restoring . . . the individual and collective responsibility we used to owe to each other," of finding the missing glue of social cohesion.

These themes and principles add up to the notion of civil society, an attractive concept at a time when many have come to fear that we are living in an increasingly uncivil society, one threatening to deteriorate into something resembling the state of nature—what Germans call "the elbow society."[19] It is possible to see the elements of civil society not only in mentoring but in a range of other extremely popular programs on the policy landscape: youth service, family support, and intergenerational and cooperative education efforts, to name a few.

These elements touch an upwelling sentiment in the contemporary United States, one concerned with resurrecting and preserving a set of social relationships perceived to be vanishing: ties between the generations, responsibility to strangers, a sense of community, and the bonds of family.

As the broad appeal of mentoring and related efforts suggests, the notion of a civil society sells. It is a pitch that might well be used more aggressively, alongside prevailing arguments concerning the social costs of neglect. Taken together, these approaches could produce a case capable of transcending customary political divisions, and of helping to rally the public will so essential to genuine reform.[20]

10

Reinventing Community

Anyone who claims that I am a dreamer who expects to transform hell into heaven is wrong. I have few illusions. . . . There is only one thing I will not concede: that it might be meaningless to strive in a good cause.

—Václav Havel,

Summer Meditations

*V*oluntary movements are as important for what they express symbolically as for what they actually address programmatically. They tell a rich story about who we are as a people, how we see our social problems, and where we are headed in the future. Mentoring is particularly rich in this respect: it has three different stories to tell.

The first is a tale of heroics, about our recurring appetite for simple, dramatic solutions to complex social problems, a fever that rises and falls but that has long been with us in American social policy. In this narrative, mentoring is portrayed as a low-cost, high-yield solution to the problems confronting young people in poverty; it features middle-class adults — expected in the millions — in the role of child savers.

This story argues that voluntarism will not only save impoverished children from the perils of their environment but also the American people from the evils of public institutions — those expensive villains that have robbed us, in Ronald Reagan's words, of "many things we once considered were really ours to do voluntarily out of the goodness of our hearts." This characterization recalls Friendly Visiting's slogan, "Not Alms, But a Friend," with its anachronistic faith in the sufficiency of well-meaning volunteers. In the case of mentoring it is built around the outlook of "fervor without infrastructure."

In place of "fervor without infrastructure," the preceding chapters have offered an alternative story. They argue that there is recourse from the overselling — and the consequential undermining — of mentoring. Through responsible practice, sufficient resources, and realistic expectations, movements like mentoring can be sustained and constructive additions to the landscape, joining a tradition carried on by sturdy efforts like those of Big Brothers/Big Sisters. Within limits already suggested, mentoring can engage a new cadre of adults on behalf of our nation's most vulnerable youth.

But there is more to this story. At their best, volunteer movements not only augment direct assistance to the disadvantaged but serve as catalysts for more encompassing reforms. Mentoring illustrates how these efforts can highlight needed institutional changes, provide models for what future changes might look like, and even help build a constituency for public improvements. As Margaret Weir of the Brookings Institution writes, such initiatives can "not only prepare the ground for major shifts" in policy "but may also chart the direction of those transformations by providing working examples of new policy and creating new conceptions about what is possible and desirable."[1]

While these two stories constitute the major focus of this book, there is yet a third, more subtle story circulating through the narrative, remaining for the most part just below the surface. This underlying tale is one of community — of the ties we have lost and the desire for new ones. Within communities, we've witnessed the withering away of civil society, of the developmental infrastructure so essential for the nurturance and socialization of future generations. Between communities, there is a widening gulf between the inner city and the rest of the United States.

John Gardner writes that the disintegration of human communities is as old as human history. He reminds us, however, that so is the recreation of human communities, that we are "a community-building species."[2] This impulse will be challenged in the future as never before. The forces pulling us apart at every level seem almost inexorable, yet at the same time our social instincts continue to function. These instincts are made visible in and strengthened by mentoring. Mentoring brings us together — across generation, class, and often race — in a manner that forces us to acknowledge our interdependence, to appreciate, in Martin Luther King, Jr.'s words, that "we are caught in an inescapable network of mutuality, tied to a single garment of destiny."[3]

In this way, mentoring enables us to participate in the essential but unfinished drama of reinventing community, while reaffirming that there is an important role for each of us in it.

Notes

Chapter One

1. Gilliam, D. "Who Will Answer the SOS?" *Washington Post,*
   Apr. 20, 1989, p. D3.
2. Terry, D. "Tug-of-War for Black Youths' Hearts." *New York
   Times,* Apr. 16, 1989, p. 26.
3. Mahoney, M. "Mentors," in the annual report of the Commonwealth Fund, New York, 1983, p. 4.
4. The William T. Grant Foundation Commission on Work,
   Family and Citizenship. *The Forgotten Half: Pathways to Success for America's Youth and Young Families.* Washington, D.C.:
   William T. Grant Foundation Commission, 1988, p. 45.
5. "Mathilda Cuomo Launches 'Year of the Mentor.'" *Alliance: The Newsletter of Governor Mario M. Cuomo's School and
   Business Alliance,* Spring/Summer 1989, p. 1.

6. Quoted in M. Marriott, "Matching Those Who Need Guidance with Those Who Have Been There." *New York Times,* Jun. 27, 1990, p. B6.

7. Quotes and information from materials provided by Project ASPIRE, Woodward High School, 7001 Reading Rd., Cincinnati, Ohio 45237.

8. "More Contagion: Project Mentor Is a Model for the Nation." Supplement to the *Atlantic Monthly,* Jul. 1990, pp. 26–27.

9. "Rhode Island Program Targets at-Risk Students." *Special Report on Mentoring,* PLUS and the National Urban League, 1990.

10. "Mentoring: The Next Generation of Philadelphians Needs Help—Maybe from You." *Philadelphia Inquirer,* Dec. 16, 1989, p. 10A.

11. Marriott, "Matching Those Who Need Guidance," p. B6.

12. Marbella, J. "RAISE Brings Mentors and Kids Together." *Baltimore Sun,* Oct. 15, 1990, p. D1.

Chapter Two

1. Concept paper, One to One, Washington, D.C., Jan. 17, 1991.

2. Dole, E. Remarks prepared for delivery, National Mentoring Conference, Washington, D.C., Mar. 28, 1990. *News,* U.S. Department of Labor, Office of Information.

3. Lautenberg, F. R. "Mentoring Can Help Us Mend Our Damaged Social Fabric." *Philadelphia Inquirer,* Sept. 8, 1992.

4. Mahoney, "Mentors," p. 5.

5. Quoted in *Mentoring: A Sound Investment in America's Future.* Pittsburgh: QED Communications, 1991, p. 5.

6. Remarks by T. W. Moloney, senior vice president, the Commonwealth Fund, to the National Mentoring Conference, Washington, D.C., Mar. 28, 1990. Transcript provided by Project Literacy U.S.

7. Remarks by F. Newman, president of the Education Commission of the States, to the National One to One Mentoring conference, Washington, D.C., Nov. 26, 1990.

8. "Dole Issues Mentoring Challenge: Businesses Should Involve at Least 10 Percent." *Work America,* May 1990.
9. Philadelphia Action Plan, One to One, May 21, 1990.
10. Gaines-Carter, P. "Turning Young Lives Around." *Washington Post,* Jun. 27, 1989, p. A1.
11. "Conclusion: Evelyn's Story." *Partnerships for Success: A Mentoring Program Manual,* joint publication of the Enterprise Foundation and the United Way of America, 1990, pp. 61–62.
12. Santiago, C. "His Brother's Keeper." *Oakland Tribune,* Jun. 16, 1992, p. B1.
13. Collins, E. G., and Scott, P. "Everyone Who Makes It Has a Mentor." *Harvard Business Review,* Jul./Aug. 1978, pp. 89–101.
14. Biesecker, K. "Mentor, Inc.: The Pied Piper of Success." *Sun Gazette,* Washington, D.C., Jan. 24, 1990.
15. *Guide to Workplace Mentoring Programs.* Washington, D.C.: One to One Partnership, 1992, p. 34.
16. "You Have the Power to Change a Life." Advertisement, *Philadelphia Inquirer,* Apr. 25, 1991.
17. Evans, T. W. *Mentors: Making a Difference in Our Public Schools.* Princeton, N.J.: Peterson's Guides, p. 3.
18. Materials provided by Fannie Mae.
19. "An Interview with New York's First Lady, Mathilda Cuomo." *Alliance,* Spring 1988, p. 4.
20. *Mentoring: A Sound Investment in America's Future,* p. 3.
21. Philadelphia Action Plan, One to One, May 21, 1990.
22. Newman, F. "Four Quick Fixes for Our Schools." *New York Times,* Apr. 15, 1990.
23. "One to One." Materials provided by One to One, p. 3.
24. "Fund Created to Help Kids Invest in Their Future." *Chronicle of Philanthropy,* Apr. 21, 1992, p. 12.
25. Lautenberg, *Philadelphia Inquirer,* Sept. 8, 1992.
26. Brochure from Philadelphia Futures, 230 S. Broad St., Philadelphia, Pa., 19102.
27. Brochure from Mentors, Inc., 5111 16th St. NW, Washington, D.C., 20011.
28. "Brother, Can You Spare Some Time?" *Philadelphia Inquirer Magazine,* Apr. 28, 1991, p. 13.

Chapter Three

Epigraph: Gurteen, S. H. *Handbook of Charity Organization.* Buffalo, New York: Published by the author, 1882, pp. 174–186.

1. In general, the discussion of Friendly Visiting draws heavily on the following sources: Lubove, R. *The Professional Altruist: The Emergence of Social Work as a Career, 1880–1930.* Cambridge, Mass.: Harvard University Press, 1965; Boyer, P. *Urban Masses and Moral Order in America, 1820–1920.* Cambridge, Mass.: Harvard University Press, 1978.; and Katz, M. *In the Shadow of the Poorhouse: A Social History of Welfare in America.* New York: Basic Books, 1986.

2. Gurteen, *Handbook,* p. 38.

3. Gurteen, *Handbook,* p. 11.

4. National Conference of Charities and Correction, *Proceedings.* Boston, Mass., 1887, pp. 132–133.

5. Gurteen, *Handbook,* p. 22.

6. Lubove, *The Professional Altruist,* p. 150.

7. Richmond, M. *Friendly Visiting Among the Poor: A Handbook for Charity Workers.* Montclair, N.J.: PattersonSmith, [1899] 1969.

8. Associated Charities of Boston, *Seventh Annual Report,* Nov. 1886, p. 9.

9. Quoted in Katz, *In the Shadow of the Poorhouse,* p. 165.

10. Boyer, *Urban Masses,* p. 155.

11. Lubove, *The Professional Altruist,* p. 23.

12. Described in G. L. Beiswinger, *One to One: The Story of the Big Brothers/Big Sisters Movement in America.* Philadelphia: Big Brothers/Big Sisters of America, 1985, pp. 34–35.

13. Cooper, C. C. "Mentors Can Serve Black Youth in Many Ways." *Journal of Negro Education,* 1985, *54*(2), p. 157; E. P. Shapiro, F. P. Haseltine, and M. P. Rowe, "Moving Up: Role Models, Mentors and the 'Patron-System,'" *Sloan Management Review,* 1978, *19*(3), pp. 51–58; Levinson, D., and others, *The Seasons of a Man's Life.* New York: Knopf, 1978.

14. Cited in S. F. Hamilton, *Apprenticeship for Adulthood.* New York: Free Press, 1990, p. 156.

15. Homer, *The Odyssey.* (E. V. Rieu, trans.) New York: Penguin Books, 1946, pp. 37–51.

16. Bly's translation of the Grimms' fairytale is presented in *Iron John: A Book About Men.* Reading, Mass.: Addison-Wesley, 1990, pp. 250–259. The original story by Jacob and Wilhelm Grimm is in *Grimms Marchen,* Zurich Manesse Verlag, 1946.

17. Raines, H. "A Mentor's Presence." *New York Times Magazine,* Jul. 20, 1986, p. 46.

18. Levinson and others, *The Seasons of a Man's Life,* pp. 333–334.

19. Interview with Robert Bly in B. Moyers, *A World of Ideas.* Vol. 2: *Public Opinions from Private Citizens.* New York: Doubleday, 1990, pp. 278–279.

20. Erikson, E., Erikson, J., and Kivniok, H. *Vital Involvements in Old Age.* New York: W. W. Norton, 1986; also see Goleman, D. "Erikson, in His Own Old Age, Expands His View of Life." *New York Times,* Jun. 14, 1989.

21. Merriam, S. "Mentors and Protégés: A Critical Review of the Literature." *Adult Education Quarterly,* 1983, *33*(3).

22. Cox, C. M. "The Early Mental Traits of Three Hundred Geniuses." In L. M. Terman, *Genetic Studies of Genius,* Vol. 2. Stanford, Calif.: Stanford University Press.; Zuckerman, H. *Scientific Elite: Nobel Laureates in the United States.* New York: Macmillan, 1977.

23. Merriam, "Mentors and Protégés," p. 169.

24. Collins, E. G., and Scott, P. "Everyone Who Makes It Has a Mentor." *Harvard Business Review,* Jul./Aug. 1978, pp. 89–101.

25. Kanter, R. M. *Men and Women of the Corporation.* New York: Basic Books, 1977.; R. M. Kanter and B. Stein, "The Gender Pioneers: Women in an Industrial Sales Force," in Kanter and Stein (eds.), *Life in Organizations.* New York: Basic Books, 1979.

26. Missirian, A. *The Corporate Connection: Why Executive Women Need Mentors to Reach the Top.* Englewood Cliffs, N.J.: Prentice-Hall, 1982.

27. Hennig, M., and Jardim, A. *The Managerial Woman.* New York: Doubleday, 1977, p. 162.

28. Phillips-Jones, L. *Mentors and Protégés: How to Establish, Strengthen and Get the Most from a Mentor/Protégé Relationship.* New York: Arbor House, 1982.

Chapter Four

Epigraph: *A Special Report on Mentoring.* Pittsburgh: Project PLUS and the Aspira Association, 1990.

1. Cited in *Interchange,* Center for Intergenerational Learning, Temple University, Fall 1992. See also Hamburg, D. A. *Preparing for Life: The Critical Transition of Adolescence.* New York: Carnegie Corporation, 1986.

2. Steinberg, L. "The Logic of Adolescence." In P. Edelman and J. Ladner (eds.), *Adolescence and Poverty: Challenge for the 1990s.* Washington, D.C.: Center for National Policy Press, 1991, p. 27.

3. Coleman, J. S. "Families and Schools." *Educational Researcher,* Aug.-Sept. 1987, pp. 32-39.

4. U.S. Department of Education, Office of Educational Research and Improvement, National Center for Educational Statistics, *National Educational Longitudinal Study of 1988: A Profile of the American Eighth-Grader.* Washington, D.C.: U.S. Government Printing Office, 1990, pp. 50-54.

5. Goleman, D. "Attending to the Children of All the World's War Zones." *New York Times,* Dec. 6, 1992; Garbarino, J., Dubrow, N., Kostelny, K., and Pardo, C. *Children in Danger: Coping with the Consequences of Community Violence.* San Francisco: Jossey-Bass, 1992.

6. See Wilson, W. J. *The Truly Disadvantaged: The Inner-City, the Underclass, and Public Policy.* Chicago: University of Chicago Press, 1987.

7. Gross, J. "Collapse of Inner-City Families Creates America's New Orphans." *New York Times,* Mar. 29, 1992.

8. Garbarino and others, *Children in Danger.*

9. Wilson, *The Truly Disadvantaged.*

10. Anderson, E. *Streetwise: Race, Class, and Change in an Urban Community.* Chicago: University of Chicago Press, 1990, p. 69.

11. Duneier, M. *Slim's Table: Race, Respectability, and Masculinity.* Chicago: University of Chicago Press, 1992, p. 111.

12. Comer, J. "Preface: A Growing Crisis in Youth Development." In *A Matter of Time: Risk and Opportunity in the Nonschool Hours,* Report of the Task Force on Youth De-

velopment and Community Programs. New York: Carnegie Corporation, 1992, p. 19.

13. West, C. "Nihilism in Black America." *Dissent,* Spring 1991, p. 223.

14. Quoted in B. Barol, "The Eighties Are Over." *Newsweek,* Jan. 4, 1988, p. 48. Additional examples of this perspective can be found in Phillips, K. *The Politics of Rich and Poor.* New York: Random House, 1990.; and Katz, M. B. *The Undeserving Poor: From the War on Poverty to the War on Welfare.* New York: Pantheon, 1989.

15. Buckley, W. F., Jr. *Gratitude.* New York: Random House, 1990, p. 60.

16. Teltsch, K. "'Baby Boomers' Increase Donations, Survey Says." *New York Times;* see also Goleman, D. "Compassionand Comfort in Middle Age: New Research Finds a Flowering of Lives, Marked by Generosity and Deeper Relationships." *New York Times,* Feb. 6, 1990, p. C14.

17. de Tocqueville, A. "Of Individualism in Democracies." In J. P. Mayer (ed.), *Democracy in America,* Vol. 2. (G. Lawrence, trans.) New York: Doubleday, Anchor Books, 1969, pp. 506–508.

18. Rowe, J. "Rebuilding the Nonmarket Economy." *The American Prospect,* Winter 1993.

19. Bellah, R. N., and others. *Habits of the Heart: Individualism and Commitment in American Life.* New York: HarperCollins, 1986, pp. 290–291.

20. Goleman, D. "Compassion and Comfort in Middle Age," p. C14.

21. Beldon and Russonello, *A Report on Baby Boomer Attitudes,* 1989. 1436 U St. NW, Washington, D.C., 20009.

22. Mahoney, "Mentors"; and H. Howe II, Speech to the National School Volunteer Conference of the National Association of Partners in Education, Baltimore, Md., Mar. 21, 1989.

23. Lee, F. R. "Trying Times for Guidance Counselors." *New York Times,* Feb. 12, 1990.

24. Task Force on Youth Development and Community Programs, *A Matter of Time,* p. 78.

25. Lemann, N. "Healing the Ghettos." *Atlantic,* Mar. 1991, p. 20.

26. "New PBS Project Literacy U.S. Special, One PLUS One, Focuses on Mentoring." Press Release from Project Literacy U.S., 1989.

27. "Philadelphia Futures Makes It Easy to Make a Difference in One Kid's Life." Philadelphia Futures brochure.

28. McGuinness, A. "In the Public Service." *Princeton Alumni Weekly,* Feb. 19, 1992, p. 7.

29. Wuthnow, R. *Acts of Compassion: Caring for Others and Helping Ourselves.* Princeton, N.J.: Princeton University Press, 1991, p. 191.

Chapter Five

Epigraph: Clinton, B. "Education and Repairing the Family." *New Perspectives Quarterly,* Fall 1990, p. 12.

1. Werner, E. E., and Smith, R. S. *Vulnerable but Invincible: A Study of Resilient Children.* New York: McGraw-Hill, 1982.

2. Garmezy, N., and Neuchterlein, K. "Invulnerable Children: the Fact and Fiction of Competence and Disadvantage." *American Journal of Orthopsychiatry,* 1972, *42.*

3. Garmezy, N. "Stress Resistant Children: The Search for Protective Factors." In J. E. Stevenson (ed.), *Recent Research in Developmental Psychopathology.* Oxford: Pergamon, 1985.

4. Rutter, M., and Giller, H. *Juvenile Delinquency: Trends and Perspectives.* New York: Guilford Press, 1983.

5. Werner and Smith, *Vulnerable but Invincible.* See also Werner, E. E. "Children of the Garden Island." *Scientific American,* Apr. 1989, p. 111.

6. "Girls at 11: An Interview with Carol Gilligan." *Harvard Education Letter,* Jul.–Aug. 1990, p. 6.

7. M. Rutter, "Psychosocial Resilience and Protective Mechanisms." *American Journal of Orthopsychiatry,* 1987, *57,* p. 57.

8. Ainsworth, M. "Attachments Beyond Infancy." *American Psychologist,* 1989, *44,* p. 709.

9. Bandura, A. "Social-Learning Theory of Identification

Processes." In D. A. Goslin (ed.), *Handbook of Socialization Theory and Research.* Chicago: Rand-McNally, 1969.

10. Caplan, G. *Principles of Preventive Psychiatry.* New York: Basic Books, 1964.

11. Williams, T., and Kornblum, W. *Growing Up Poor.* New York: Lexington Books, 1985, p. 108.

12. Lefkowitz, B. *Tough Change: Growing Up on Your Own in America.* New York: Free Press, 1986.

13. Rhodes, J. "Older and Wiser: Mentoring Relationships in Childhood and Adolescence." Unpublished paper, University of Illinois, 1992.

14. Cave, G., and Quint, J. *Career Beginnings Impact Evaluation: Findings from a Program for Disadvantaged High School Students.* New York: Manpower Demonstration Research Corporation, 1990.

15. McPartland, J., and Nettles, S. "Using Community Adults as Advocates or Mentors for At-Risk Middle School Students: A Two-Year Evaluation of Project RAISE." *American Journal of Education,* Aug. 1991.

16. Stanwyck, D. J., and Anson, C. A. *The Adopt-a-Student Evaluation Project: Final Report.* Atlanta: Department of Educational Foundations, Georgia State University, 1989.

17. Task Force on Youth Development and Community Programs, *A Matter of Time,* p. 11.

18. Bronfenbrenner, U. "Alienation and the Four Worlds of Childhood." *Phi Delta Kappan,* Feb. 1986, p. 430.

19. Ferguson, R. F. *The Case for Community-Based Programs That Inform and Motivate Black Male Youth.* Washington, D.C.: The Urban Institute, 1990, p. 13.

20. Garbarino and others, *Children in Danger,* p. 118.

21. Werner, E. E. "Protective Factors and Individual Resilience." In S. J. Meisels and J. P. Shonkoff (eds.), *Handbook of Early Childhood Education.* Cambridge, England: Cambridge University Press, 1990, p. 111.

Chapter Six

1. McPartland and Nettles, "Using Community Adults," p. 568.

2. Hamilton, S., and Hamilton, M. A. "Mentoring Programs: Promise and Paradox." *Phi Delta Kappan,* Mar. 1992, p. 546.
3. Ferguson, *The Case for Community-Based Programs,* p. 15.
4. Tierney, J. P., and Branch, A. Y. *College Students and Mentors for At-Risk Youth: A Study of Six Campus Partners in Learning Programs.* Philadelphia: Public/Private Ventures, 1992.
5. Hamilton and Hamilton, "Mentoring Programs," p. 546.
6. Schor, J. B. *The Overworked American: The Unexpected Decline of Leisure.* New York: Basic Books, 1991.
7. Kuttner, R. "No Time to Smell the Roses Anymore." *New York Times Book Review,* Feb. 2, 1992, p. 1.
8. Flaxman, E., Ascher, C., and Harrington, C. *Youth Mentoring Programs and Practices.* New York: Institute for Urban and Minority Education, Teachers College, Columbia University, 1988, p. 3.
9. *The MEE Report: Reaching the Hip-Hop Generation.* Philadelphia: MEE Productions, 1992, p. xii.
10. Goleman, D. "Black Scientists Study the 'Pose' of the Inner City." *New York Times,* Apr. 21, 1992, p. C1.
11. Ahlgren, P. "New Project Gets So-So Grades: Mentor Program Fails to Raise Most Pupils' Performance." *Milwaukee Journal,* Aug. 20, 1989.
12. McPartland and Nettles, "Using Community Adults," p. 568.
13. Memo from management to board, Project RAISE, 1990.
14. Flaxman and Ascher, "Mentoring Programs and Practices."
15. Schuldt, G. "Mentors Help At-Risk Students, but Program No Panacea." *Milwaukee Sentinel,* Mar. 21, 1990.
16. O'Boyle, T. F. "Mentor-Protégé Ties Can Be Strained." *Wall Street Journal,* Jun. 12, 1990, p. B1.
17. Merriam, "Mentors and Protégés."
18. Healy, C., and Welchert, A. "Mentoring Relations: A Definition to Advance Research and Practice." *Educational Researcher,* Dec. 1990, p. 19.
19. "Both Sides Win with Mentoring." *USA Today,* Mar. 29, 1990.
20. *Youth Investment and Community Reconstruction: Street Lessons on Drugs and Crime for the Nineties, A Tenth Anniversary Report of the Milton S. Eisenhower Foundation.* Washington, D.C.: The Eisenhower Foundation, 1990.

21. See. G. Walker and F. Vilella-Velez, *Anatomy of a Demonstration.* Philadelphia: Public/Private Ventures, 1992.

22. Garbarino and others, *Children in Danger,* p. 118.

Chapter Seven

1. Ahlgren, "New Project Gets So-So Grades."

2. Gilliam, D. "Mentoring Has Its Limitations." *Washington Post,* Apr. 9, 1990.

3. *Turning Point: A White Paper on the Course of Mentoring.* Pittsburgh: PLUS/WQED, 1990, p. 12.

4. The following titles provide a sampling of these manuals: The National Mentoring Working Group, *Mentoring: Elements of Effective Practice.* Washington, D.C.: United Way of America, 1990.; Abell Foundation, *Mentoring Manual: A Guide to Program Development and Implementation.* Baltimore: Abell Foundation, 1989.; Abell Foundation, *The Two of Us: A Handbook for Mentors.* Baltimore: Abell Foundation, 1991.; United Way of America and the Enterprise Foundation, *Partnerships for Success: A Mentoring Program Manual.* Alexandria, Va.: United Way of America, and Columbia, Md.: Enterprise Foundation, 1990.; Campus Partners in Learning, *Resource Manual for Campus-Based Mentoring Programs for At-Risk Youth.* Providence, R.I.: Campus Compact, 1990.; and U.S. Department of Education, *One on One: A Guide to Establishing Mentor Programs.* Washington, D.C.: USDOE, forthcoming.

5. See Freedman, M. *Partners in Growth.* Philadelphia: Public/Private Ventures, 1988. See also Mincey, R., "Proposal for Minority Male Conference Grant." Washington, D.C.: The Urban Institute, 1991.

6. Ferguson, *The Case for Community-Based Programs,* p. 11.

7. Quoted in Urban Strategies Council, *Connections,* p. 26.

8. Hamilton and Hamilton, "Mentoring Programs."

9. This section draws heavily on F. Kanfer, S. Englund, C. Lenhoff, and J. Rhodes, *Mentor Manual and Facts Sheets.* Urbana-Champaign: University of Illinois, Department of Psychology, 1992, p. 70; and on M. B. Styles and K. V. Morrow, *Understanding How Youth and Elders Form Rela-*

tionships: A Study of Four Linking Lifetimes Programs. Philadelphia: Public/Private Ventures, 1992, p. iii.

10. Flaxman, E., and Ascher, C. *Mentoring in Action: The Efforts of Programs in New York City.* New York: Institute for Urban and Minority Education, Teachers College, Columbia University, 1992, p. 10.

Chapter Eight

1. The phrase "mentor-rich environments" derives from the Uncommon Individual Foundation in Radnor, Pa.
2. Glazer, N. *The Limits of Social Policy.* Cambridge, Mass.: Harvard University Press, 1988, p. 146.
3. Ferguson, *The Case for Community-Based Programs,* p. 11.
4. Sommerfeld, M. "Asked to 'Dream,' Students Beat the Odds." *Education Week,* Apr. 8, 1992.
5. Anderson, *Streetwise,* p. 107.
6. Howe, H. II, Speech to the National School Volunteer Conference of the National Association of Partners in Education, Baltimore, Md., Mar. 21, 1989.
7. "A Caring Adult for Every Child." *California Tomorrow,* Sept. 1990.
8. Garbarino and others, *Children in Danger,* pp. 145–147.
9. Hamburg, D. A. *Early Adolescence: A Critical Time for Interpretations in Education and Health.* New York: Carnegie Corporation, 1989.
10. Quoted in Ferguson, *The Case for Community-Based Programs,* p. 10.
11. Cited in L. Schorr with D. Schorr, *Within Our Reach: Breaking the Cycle of Disadvantage.* New York: Doubleday, 1988, pp. 226–227.
12. Dryfoos, J. *Adolescents At-Risk: Prevention and Prevalence.* New York: Oxford University Press, 1990, p. 241.
13. Csikszentmihalyi, M., and McCormack, J. "The Influence of Teachers." *Phi Delta Kappan,* Feb. 1986, p. 418.
14. Lightfoot, S. L. *The Good High School: Portraits of Character and Culture.* New York: Basic Books, 1983, p. 323.
15. Bryk, A. S., and Driscoll, M. E. *The High School as Com-*

munity: Contextual Influences and Consequences for Students and Teachers. Report from the National Center on Effective Secondary Schools, Madison, Wis., Nov. 1988.

16. *Voices from the Inside.* Report from the Institute for Education in Transformation, Claremont Graduate School, 1992.; see also Rothman, R. "Study 'from Inside' Finds a Deeper Set of School Problems." *Education Week,* Dec. 2, 1992, p. 9.

17. Edwards, T. K. "Providing Reasons for Wanting to Live." *Phi Delta Kappan,* Dec. 1988, p. 297.

18. Articles around the country describing this trend include the following: "Trying Times for Guidance Counselors." *New York Times,* Feb. 12, 1990.; D. Curtis, "Crisis for School Counselors: Budget Pressures Mean More Work for Fewer Student Advisers." *San Francisco Chronicle,* May 8, 1991.; "S.F. School Board Cuts 165 Positions." *San Francisco Chronicle,* Sept. 14, 1991.

Chapter Nine

1. Healy and Welchert, "Mentoring Relations," p. 17.

2. Quoted in A. Wolfe, "The New American Dilemma." *The New Republic,* Apr. 13, 1992, p. 30.

3. Reich, R. *The Work of Nations.* New York: Knopf, 1991.

4. Quoted in P. Applebome, "Although Urban Blight Worsens, Most People Don't Feel Its Impact." *New York Times,* Jan. 28, 1991, p. 1.

5. Fallows, J. *More Like Us.* Boston: Houghton Mifflin, 1989, p. 175.

6. Gray, J. "Peace Corps Training Uses Camden Schools." *New York Times,* Nov. 9, 1992, p. B5.

7. Kotlowitz, A. *There Are No Children Here.* New York: Doubleday, 1991, pp. 6–7.

8. Slater, P. *The Pursuit of Loneliness.* Boston: Beacon Press, 1970, p. 19.

9. "Bennett Suggests Orphanages as Drug Refuge." Associated Press, Apr. 27, 1990.

10. Applebome, "Although Urban Blight Worsens," p. 1.

11. Cited in J. DeParle, "On the Edge of Innocence: Waiting for a New Dickens." *New York Times,* Sept. 1, 1991, p. 4.

12. Taylor, P. "Plight of Children: Seen but Unheeded." *Washington Post,* Jul. 5, 1991, p. A4.

13. "Child Watch Visitation Program." Project description, Children's Defense Fund, Washinton, D.C., 1991.

14. Katz, M. B. *In the Shadow of the Poorhouse: A Social History of Welfare in America.* New York: Basic Books, 1986.

15. Lasch, C. *The True and Only Heaven: Progress and Its Critics.* New York: Norton, 1991, p. 36.

16. Interview with Mary Catherine Bateson in B. Moyers, *A World of Ideas.* New York: Doubleday, 1989, p. 346.

17. Graham, P. A. "Business and the Schools." *Daedalus,* Spring 1990.

18. Smothers, R. "Carter's Civic Crusade Tries to Meld Two Atlantas." *New York Times,* Apr. 11, 1992, p. 6.

19. On the loss of civil society and its importance, a number of recent writings are appropriate: Wolfe, A. *Whose Keeper? Social Science and Moral Obligation.* Berkeley and Los Angeles: University of California Press, 1989.; Gitlin, T. "The Uncivil Society." *New Perspectives Quarterly,* Spring 1990.; Glendon, M. A. *Rights Talk: The Impoverishment of Political Discourse.* New York: Free Press, 1991.; and West, C. "Nihilism in Black America." *Dissent,* Spring 1991.

20. This position is articulated by Heather B. Weiss in her article "Beyond Parens Patriae: Building Policies and Programs to Care for Our Own and Others' Children." *Children and Youth Services Review,* 1990, *12*(3).

Chapter Ten

1. Weir, M. *Politics and Jobs: The Boundaries of Employment Policy in the United States.* Princeton: Princeton University Press, 1992, p. 176.

2. Gardner, J. W. *Building Community.* Washington, D.C.: The Independent Sector, 1991, p. 9.

3. King, M. L., Jr. "Letter from the Birmingham Jail, Alabama, 16 April 1963." *Atlantic Monthly,* Aug. 1963, p. 81.

Index